Mustang and Thunderbolt Aces of the Pacific and CBI

SERIES EDITOR: TONY HOLMES

OSPREY AIRCRAFT OF THE ACES • 26

Mustang and Thunderbolt Aces of the Pacific and CBI

John Stanaway

Front cover
The Fifth Air Force produced just one Mustang ace during World War 2, but he did down seven of his eight kills in a solitary sortie! On the morning of 11 January 1945, Capt William Shomo, CO of the 71st Tactical Reconnaissance Group's 81st Tactical Reconnaissance Squadron (TRS), and his wingman, Lt Paul Lipscomb, were on an armed recce to Atarri and Laoag airstrips on the large Philippine island of Luzon when a single G4M 'Betty' bomber, escorted by no fewer than 11 Ki-61s and a solitary Ki-44, was spotted through a break in thin cloud. Rushing in to engage the unsuspecting enemy, Shomo and Lipscomb hit the left formation of 'Tonys' first, downing four fighters in quick succession from close range. The former then manoeuvred his F-6D-10 (44-14841) in behind the second element on the right side, as his combat report details;

'The second element of two "Tonys" on the right side of the formation turned to the left and started after my wingman, who was moving down on the remaining element of two "Tonys" on the left side. As this element crossed over, they passed directly in front of me, and I fired a burst into the wingman and he exploded in flames. Lt Lipscomb then fired at the wingman of the first element on the left side and this "Tony" also burst into flames. Lt Lipscomb then made a pass on the bomber, but apparently did no damage. I then started to make a pass on the bomber, and as I closed on its tail from the right quarter, a rear gunner started to fire at me, so I dropped my wing tanks to be less vulnerable. I dropped below the bomber and raked the underside of the fuselage with a long burst. The right wing root caught fire and black smoke started streaming behind the bomber as I passed under and beyond it.

'I started up in a steep climb to the left, and at this point I saw my wingman's third victory as he hit a "Tony" in a head-on pass. It started to smoke and burn as it rolled into a vertical dive from about 600 ft. While still in the climbing turn, a "Tojo" started to fire at me from below, and with about 60° deflection. I tightened my climbing turn, and he skidded behind me,

broke off and disappeared into the low hanging cloud.

'By this time I was headed in the original direction of the running fight, and saw the bomber crash in the field and burst into flames. I also saw two "Tonys" in element formation, just beyond where the bomber crashed, flying south at an altitude of approximately 800 ft. I pursued them, closed on the lead "Tony", and fired a burst into him from the rear. This "Tony" exploded and broke up in mid-air. The other "Tony" broke to the right, and dove steeply to an altitude of approximately 300 ft, and as I closed on the fighter's tail, he levelled out. I closed to point-blank range and

fired a burst that started black smoke streaming from his engine exhaust stacks. I was overrunning this "Tony", so I swerved out to the right side and above him. The "Tony" went into a gentle dive toward the ground. I snapped a picture with the oblique camera mounted on the fuselage of my airplane just before the "Tony" struck the ground and burst into flame.'

William Shomo was subsequently credited with seven kills and Paul Lipscomb three, and the former pilot duly awarded the Congressional Medal of Honor for his exploits on this sortie
(*cover artwork by Iain Wyllie*)

First published in Great Britain in 1999 by Osprey Publishing
Elms Court, Chapel Way, Botley, Oxford, OX2 9LP

ISBN 1 85532 780 5

Edited by Tony Holmes
Page design by TT Designs, T & B Truscott
Cover Artwork by Iain Wyllie
Aircraft Profiles by Tom Tullis
Figure Artwork by Mike Chappell (and uniform notes by I J Phillips)
Scale Drawings by Mark Styling

Origination by Valhaven Ltd, Isleworth, UK
Printed through Bookbuilders, Hong Kong

99 00 01 02 03   10 9 8 7 6 5 4 3 2 1

ACKNOWLEDGEMENTS
The following individuals kindly gave me their views and descriptions of flying either the P-47 or P-51 in the Pacific and CBI – Carl Fischer, Santiago Flores, Don Lopez, Jim Tapp, Lawrence O'Neill, Ralph Wandrey and Wallace Jordan. Other researchers and historians who 'helped with the cause' included Dr Bill Wolf, Jim Lansdale, Larry Davis, Bill Hess, Ray Toliver and Jim Crow.

CONTENTS

INTRODUCTION

Some years ago I experienced for the first time a surge of 'Mustang fever' when the orchestrated snarl of a Merlin engine shook our building just off Wittman Field in Oshkosh, Wisconsin. There was no mistaking the identity of the Air Adventure Museum's P-51D, and I knew then why so many people felt a reverence for the aeroplane. Sometime soon after World War 2, I had watched returning P-47s in formation and felt a similar thrill at the power and beauty of their flight. Indeed, it seems impossible to watch either of these fighter types take to the skies without being stirred.

The combat record for each of these aircraft is beyond criticism in the European Theatre of Operations (ETO). Almost 5000 enemy aircraft fell to Mustang pilots, while their compatriots in the Thunderbolt were credited with over 3000 kills. Hundreds of pilots became aces flying these two types, with many more achieving notable successes against aircraft on the ground. Troops, trucks, tanks and any other worthwhile targets also suffered heavily at the hands of P-47 and P-51 pilots during the final stages of the war, units sweeping unmolested across occupied territory at tree-top level.

However, combat in the Pacific required the two fighter types to prove themselves again, with sometimes mixed results. Just as the P-38 had been dominant in the Pacific and Mediterranean theatres prior to it being required to acquit itself in the damp, thin air of northern Europe, so the Mustang and Thunderbolt had to adjust to the conditions of battle in the Pacific.

The P-47 was especially despised in the early days of the campaign because of its short range and mediocre low altitude performance. Indeed, the Thunderbolt's potential was not fully realised until Col Neel Kearby arrived in the Southwest Pacific with his 348th Fighter Group (FG) in mid-1943. Despite being new to combat himself, Kearby was nonetheless a seasoned Thunderbolt pilot, and he used his experience of the big fighter to develop the high-level sweep and slashing diving attack, which made maximum use of the aircraft's major advantage over its Japanese rivals – its high diving speed. This tactic would be employed with great effect by all P-47 groups across the Pacific until war's end.

Convinced of the fighter's ability, Kearby set about ensuring that at least half the squadrons within V Fighter Command (FC) operated Thunderbolts for at least part of 1944, and by the end of the war in excess of 20 pilots within the command had scored five or more aerial kills with the P-47.

Fortune was little kinder to the Mustang during its opening months in combat, since the first model to see action was the Allison-powered P-51A. Despite being much faster than the Ki-43 Hayabusa ('Oscar'), which at that time was it main rival, a number of Mustangs were lost early on when inexperienced American pilots failed to heed the warnings of their predecessors about attempting to turn with the more agile Japanese fighters. However, once this tactical error was realised, the P-51A soon proved itself in combat, with pilots like Jim England (eight kills in A-models) and Bob Mulhollem (five kills) having made 'ace' over Burma by the spring of 1944.

Things improved dramatically for the Mustang when the first P-51Bs arrived in China in mid-1944, and by 1945 the D-model had been introduced, swiftly becoming the dominant fighter type in the China-Burma-India (CBI) theatre. The P-51D also enjoyed great success in the Central Pacific during long bomber escort missions to the Japanese home islands, although it failed to dislodge the P-38 from its position of dominance within the Fifth Air Force.

Perhaps the greatest success enjoyed by the P-47 and P-51 in operations against the Japanese came with units assigned to the Seventh Air Force (also in the Central Pacific). No fewer than ten pilots from that air force scored five or more victories, and the Seventh was the only AAF unit to regularly escort heavy bombers sent to attack the Japanese mainland.

This volume deals with the aces who flew Thunderbolts or Mustangs (and, on the rare occasion, both types) in the Pacific and CBI. Fittingly, the ranking pilot was Medal of Honor recipient Col Neel Kearby, who claimed 22 aerial victories whilst proving the worth of the big Republic fighter in-theatre. Other high-scoring P-47 pilots included Maj William 'Dinghy' Dunham with 15 (plus one with the P-51K) and Col Bob Rowland with nine. Turning to the Mustang, the highest scorers were Maj John 'Pappy' Herbst and Lt Col Ed McComas of the CBI's 23rd FG, who both scored 14 victories apiece, whilst Maj Robert Moore of the 15th FG (in the Central Pacific) claimed 11 victories in the P-51.

Hardly household names, these men have often had their exploits overshadowed by Mustang and Thunderbolt pilots in the ETO, not to mention the many aces who flew the Lightning in the Pacific and CBI. With this fact in mind, I therefore hope that this volume goes some way to at last bring the achievements of these pilots to the fore.

John Stanaway
Sioux City, Iowa
February 1999

P-47 COMES TO THE PACIFIC

As briefly mentioned in the introduction to this book, Republic's P-47 Thunderbolt never won easy acceptance into combat in the Southwest Pacific theatre due to the spirited opposition provided by the primary Japanese Army and Navy fighters of the day, namely the Nakajima Ki-43 'Oscar' and the Mitsubishi A6M Zero. Most critics thought that the American fighter was simply too big and ungainly to enter into battle with even the heavier Luftwaffe fighters in the ETO, let alone their nimble Axis counterparts over the steaming jungles of New Guinea and New Britain. Furthermore, many of the group and squadron commanders within the Fifth Air Force (whose units were slated to receive the first P-47s to arrive in-theatre) saw the Thunderbolt's limited range and lack of low altitude manoeuvrability as deciding factors in rejecting the type out of hand.

However, the commander of the Fifth Air Force, Gen George Churchill Kenney, wanted every combat aircraft that he could get his hands on sent to the Pacific, and these included the P-47. He was convinced that the big fighter could be used to deadly effect in wresting aerial supremacy from the Japanese. Kenney was called 'The Operator' by his combat crews, this nickname referring to his willingness to improvise and supply his combat units with whatever aircraft he could obtain in an effort to go on the offensive against the Japanese.

Despite his willingness to utilise almost any combat type in the inventory, Kenney was also fully aware of the P-47's primary problem when it came to combat in the Pacific – its limited range. To the strategists within V FC, the Thunderbolt's modest combat radius seemed to have effectively ruled the aircraft out of the long-range penetration role. But the boss of the Fifth Air Force was not to be denied, for he desperately wanted to see his fighter groups striking deep into the heart of Japanese-held territory. The P-47 would have to succeed.

Col Neel Kearby is seen leading a flight of 348th FG P-47Ds soon after the group had arrived in New Guinea. This photograph was taken sometime in July 1943

This close-up shot was also taken on the same photo sortie as the previous image. The P-47D-2 furthest from the camera is 42-8095

Fortunately for Gen Kenney, the first Thunderbolts to reach Port Moresby in May-June 1943 were from the 348th FG, commanded by Lt Col Neel Kearby. Kenney took to the wiry young Texan on sight, and later said that, 'He looked like money in the bank to me'. He also noted that the first thing Kearby had asked him when he reported for duty was 'where could he find the Japanese?'

A skilled, if combat-inexperienced, pilot, Kearby had been flying with the Army since 1937. Prior to joining the newly-formed 348th FG as its first commanding officer in October 1942, he had accumulated hundreds of hours on P-39s undertaking mundane patrols with the 14th Pursuit Squadron/53rd Pursuit Group in the Panama Protection Zone.

As one of the first pilots within the 347th FG checked out on the 13,000-lb P-47, then-Maj Kearby was so impressed with the aircraft that he was convinced that it would prevail over any Axis fighter of the day.

Republic had taken heed of combat reports emanating from Europe in 1939-40, which categorically stated that air combat was taking placing at higher altitudes than had previously been envisaged. To survive in the ETO, the P-47 would have to achieve its optimum performance at ceilings in excess of 20,000 ft. When the fighter finally entered combat in Europe in 1943, it soon proved its worth as a bomber escort at rarefied heights (see *Aircraft of the Aces 24 - Thunderbolt Aces of the Eighth Air Force* for further details). However, it achieved this success at a price – poor manoeuvrability at low to medium altitudes, and a somewhat pedestrian rate of climb.

Aware that the P-47 was optimised for high-altitude operations, Neel Kearby devised his tactics to exploit this strength. Steadily climbing to a height of around 25,000 ft following take off from Port Moresby's Jackson Drome, Kearby would head for the distant Japanese fortress of Wewak once he had attained this pre-determined ceiling. With the enemy airfield in sight, he would dive into the airspace over the base in a 'slashing' attack, then depart for friendly territory using the speed and momentum built up during the long descent.

Numerous kills were claimed by Kearby and the 348th FG using this tactic, and the Japanese soon learned to fear the P-47, which seemed to give little warning of its presence before unleashing its massive firepower of eight .50-in guns.

The 348th FG's early successes were the direct result of Neel Kearby's careful study of the P-47 as a weapon of war. He was fully aware that the aircraft was tailored towards high-altitude combat in the ETO, and that all aerial action in the Pacific up to then had been fought at heights often well below 20,000 ft. Kearby therefore set about training his pilots to cruise at altitudes in excess of 25,000 ft so as to make maximum use of the P-47's high altitude performance and spectacular diving ability.

His tactics paid dividends right from the start, and in the first five months of combat from August through to December 1943, the group lost just eight pilots to all causes, and claimed more than 150 aerial victories.

FIRST P-47 ACES

Fittingly, the first Pacific P-47 pilot to achieve five kills was Col Neel Kearby himself, and to make this achievement even more memorable, he 'made ace' on the same mission that he received America's highest award for bravery – the Medal of Honor. He had opened his account on 4 September 1943 with a G4M 'Betty' bomber and an 'Oscar' during an interception south of Hopoi Beach, east of Lae, and he followed this double score up by downing a Ki-46 near Malahang ten days later.

Promoted to full colonel on 23 September, Kearby's next kills were claimed during the group's first independent fighter sweep of Wewak on 11 October. Arriving over the Japanese bastion late in the morning, the flight of four P-47s ran straight into a mixed formation of around 40 Army Air Force 'Oscars' and 'Tonys' that had been scrambled to intercept the raiders. In the ensuing melee, which lasted for almost an hour, Kearby was credited with four of the 'Oscars' (which he claimed as Japanese navy 'Zekes' and 'Haps') and two 'Tonys', while 341st FS Operations Officer, and future 7-kill ace, Capt John Moore, also claimed two Ki-61s to take his score three. Another future ace in Capt Bill 'Dinghy' Dunham of the 342nd FS got his first victory when he too shot down a 'Tony'.

The one-sided result of this action was quickly relayed back to Fifth Air Force commander, Gen George Kenney, who in turn immediately requested that Neel Kearby be awarded to Medal of Honor. This was duly granted on 6 January 1944, and Kenney personally presented the medal to Kearby soon afterwards.

The final mission report lodged by the 348th FG's Intelligence Officer (Lt Bernard A Roth) reveals just how pleased the group was at their CO's success, which effectively confirmed the P-47's potential in the Pacific theatre;

'The history-making aspect of this flight is unquestionable. The results obtained – Col Kearby's six victories (two "Zekes", two "Haps", two "Tonys"), Capt Moore's two "Tonys", Capt Dunham's one "Tony" – a total of nine fighters destroyed without a scratch on a single Thunderbolt, demonstrates that this type of plane has come into its own in this theatre and that its terrific speed both in the dive and straightaway, its flashing aileron roll, and murderous firepower will henceforth strike terror into the hearts of the little yellow airman.

This 340th FS P-47D-2 was the mount of future ace Lt Mike Dikovitsky, who only started scoring once he was issued with an improved D-23 in early February 1944

'In conclusion, it should be noted that this plane flew well over 300 miles, fought for one hour, and returned, the whole mission consuming about three hours and one half. About 3500 rounds of ammunition were expended, and over 100 ft of film taken.'

By the end of 1943 there were at least six P-47 pilots within the 348th FG with five or more aerial victories to their credit. Kearby was far and away the most successful pilot, having taken his score to 17 following further successes in October and December. Meanwhile, his

Lt Lawrence O'Neill pauses for a photo to send 'back home' prior to flying a mission in September 1943. The victory flag on the side of his P-47D-2 was for his first G4M 'Betty' bomber, scored on 13 September

old friend from his time in the Panama Canal, Capt Bill Dunham, had also achieved acedom following a triple score during a patrol over Arawe, on the south-west corner of the island of New Britain, on 21 December 1943. The new ace filed the following encounter report on this action;

'We took off on a scheduled eight-ship mission to patrol over shipping at Arawe. There was cloud cover at 2000 ft, beneath the overcast. We were over the target at 1605/L and patrolled until 1645, at which time we got into the fight. The Nips mixed us up at first by vectoring us to the east when everything was coming in from the west. It was very well done and fooled everybody, including the ground stations – correct code name, frequency and phrasing were used. As soon as our controller said they were being attacked, we turned around and attacked 22 dive-bombers. I attacked from the rear with three ships. My first long burst from close range set a "Val" on fire and I immediately swung onto another. He took evasive action and I kept firing. I did not observe any hits, but he crashed into the sea as I turned off.

'I then pulled out to the left and looked the situation over and attacked another "Val" from the rear. I started firing at 300 yards and closed to 25 ft. The ship started burning and crashed into the jungle. I then attacked

another ship, but due to five guns being jammed, I was unable to knock him down. I also fired at two other ships from the astern position, but couldn't knock them down. I also saw another ship crash in the jungles within a mile of my last one. It was Lt Hilbig's, as I learned later. I finally ran out of ammunition. It would have been a simple matter to knock down seven or eight if my ammunition had held out. There were Zeros above me, but Capt (William) Banks kept them occupied. I claim three "Vals" definitely destroyed.'

O'Neill proudly poses by his final victory tally of five 'Betty' bombers, four of which were scored on 26 December 1943. His combat report for this remarkable feat was frustratingly brief, stating no more than basic times and locations – and the fact that he claimed four Japanese aircraft destroyed

CO of the 342nd FS, Capt Bill Banks had claimed his fifth kill (a 'Dinah') less than 24 hours earlier north-west of Arawe, and although he had failed to score during this particular sortie, he had succeeded in preventing the marauding Zero escorts from intercepting his fellow pilots as they attacked the vulnerable 'Vals'.

Another 348th pilot who became an ace before the end of 1943 was Capt Sam Blair, the affable veteran of the 341st FS who had been with the unit right from its formation. A 1938 graduate of the University of Minnesota, he had entered the aviation cadet programme in early 1941, and received his wings just three days after the Pearl Harbor attack. Blair took his score to five with a double-kill during yet another early sweep over Arawe on 17 December 1943. His encounter report stated;

Col Neel Kearby stands by his third *Fiery Ginger IV*, alias P-47D-4 42-22668. He enjoyed much success with this aircraft, but was also ultimately shot down and killed whilst flying it

'At Arawe, about 0815/L, while our flight was at 10,000 ft, we observed (a formation of) approximately 40 enemy aircraft consisting of 15 "Oscars" and 25 "Vals". They were in "Vee" formation, at about 15,000 ft high. When first observed, they were coming from the north-east. The "Oscars" were dark green and the others were greenish brown. They had red roundels on the wings and fuselage. We dropped our belly tanks and attacked. The "Vals" started their dive on the target. We started down after them but our destroyers put up so much ack-ack that we pulled to the right and dived on the "Vals" leaving the target. I picked a flight and dived through them, indicating 400 mph.

'I pulled off and found myself alone. I spotted three more "Vals" heading north-west and made two passes at them, firing short bursts, but they took violent evasive action with short turns, and I couldn't get a good lead on any of them. I climbed and then dived on them again, started firing

Lt Col Dick Rowland's P-47D-2 42-8096, nicknamed *Miss Mutt II*/*PRIDE OF LODI OHIO*, is seen in early December 1943 after he had scored his fourth and fifth victories – two 'Hamps' downed near Saidor on 7 November

out of range at 200 ft altitude, and one of them rolled over on his back and split-essed into the trees. I pulled up and lost the others, so I headed for Arawe, climbing. I had reached 5000 ft when I spotted three "Oscars" headed north-west over the trees. I dived on them, but before I was in range, two made a tight turn to the left and the other to the right. I fired a short burst quarter head-on, but observed no results. I continued these tactics on three more passes and then I climbed up-sun to about 5000 ft. I made one more pass from this position to

P-47D-2 *Dirty Old Man* was regularly flown by Capt Walter Benz while he was part of the 342nd FS during 1943-44. It is likely that the four kill markings worn beneath the canopy of the big fighter reflect victories scored by Benz whilst flying this very machine between October and December 1943. He did not claim his fifth confirmed victory for another year. Note the distinctive flat external 200-gallon 'Brisbane' tank fitted beneath the fighter's belly, this vital piece of equipment effectively solving the range problems initially associated with the P-47 in the Southwest Pacific. The tank's name was derived from its place of invention – the capital city of Queensland, in Australia, which was also home to a large USAAF servicing depot (*Wallace*)

about 150 ft altitude, then started firing at the "Oscar" from out of range and closed up behind him. I observed strikes and he failed to pull up over a hill and crashed straight into it.'

Blair's encounter report suggests that, contrary to popular belief at the time, the P-47 was equally comfortable at both very low altitude and ceilings in excess of 20,000 ft. Always an advocate of using superior height to gain the advantage, Neel Kearby demonstrated the soundness of this doctrine yet again just 72 hours into 1944 when he led a four-fighter sweep of Wewak;

'We were over the target at 1430/L at 27,000 ft. One enemy "Zeke" (probably an "Oscar") was sighted below proceeding from But to Wewak strip at 4000 ft. I opened fire at 1000 ft from dead astern, indicating about 350 mph. I saw strikes on the fuselage, and after a three-second burst the "Zeke" burst into flames. As I passed him I turned slightly to see that he definitely went down. Instead, the fire went out and the "Zeke" continued on its course. I made a 360° turn and came in dead astern once more. No evasive action was taken by the enemy plane. I gave him a six-second burst and he again caught fire, but after I went by him the fire went out again. We were down to 1000 ft now, and when I turned to come in again the enemy plane crashed into the sea.'

This was the colonel's second kill of 3 January, for he had disposed of a Ki-21 'Sally' heavy bomber caught taking off from an airstrip during a morning sweep. Again he used superior height advantage, closing on the lumbering bomber at high speed, setting both of its engines alight, and then returning to altitude before the six enemy fighters spotted patrolling in the area could react. Kearby's flight members on both occasions were pilots 'scrounged' from the 341st FS, the colonel having by this stage been transferred to V FC Headquarters on the express orders of Gen Kenney himself.

His posting 'upstairs' had been issued on 12 November 1943, with former group executive officer Lt Col Dick Rowland being promoted to lead the wing. The latter individual was the sixth, and last, P-47 pilot to achieve ace status in 1943, claiming his fifth kill (a 'Betty') on Boxing Day

Capt Edward Roddy of the 342nd FS poses in front of his P-47D, *Babs IV*. He had claimed seven kills when this shot was take in early 1944, making him one of the 348th FG's high scorers at the time. Roddy added an eighth (and last) victory to his tally on 4 February 1944

afternoon – at roughly the same time, 342nd FS pilot Lt Lawrence O'Neill had also 'made ace' with an impressive haul of four 'Betty' bombers whilst protecting an Allied convoy from attack of Umbol Island. He had earlier claimed a solitary G4M in September 1943.

Neel Kearby, meanwhile, had soon found that his new job was not to his liking, with the dual pressures of seemingly unsolvable administrative problems and limited combat time quickly getting him down. Despite his protestations, Gen Kenney was keen to preserve leadership talent in his command, and this meant removing combat veterans from risky frontline postings in order to pass on their experience in training or planning commands. Despite Kenney effectively 'plucking' leading pilots out of the frontline, many of these individuals managed to wangle regular sorties, and consequently a number of them were lost in action – much to Kenney's dismay.

Like his contemporaries, Neel Kearby was driven by a desire to down Japanese aircraft, and he would regularly 'borrow' a P-47D from the 348th FG and lead a four-aircraft section on a sweep of his favourite 'hunting ground' over Wewak. During a press conference that he attended soon after arriving at V FC, he was asked about his allotment of combat flying hours, and he answered that he was rationed to two flights a week or less. He then added, 'The General put a lot of emphasis on that "or less"'.

By this stage, Kearby had got caught up in an unofficial USAAF 'ace race', which the press 'beat up' to raise interest back home in the 'forgotten' New Guinea theatre. Ranking American air ace Dick Bong was 'top of the pile' with 21 kills (see *Aircraft of the Aces 14 - P-38 Lightning Aces of the Pacific and CBI* for further details), although he had returned to the USA on leave in November. Fellow P-38 pilot Tom Lynch was also in America on leave, having scored 16 kills prior to his departure. This left Kearby alone in-theatre with the opportunity to overhaul Bong's score in the still somewhat unfashionable P-47. Only Gen Kenney effectively stood in his way.

Despite his stated ambition to score 50 kills before he allowed himself to be taken out of the frontline permanently, Kearby nevertheless became

Capt Sam Blair of the 341st FS was also an ace by the end of 1943, destroying six confirmed kills between October and December. His seventh, and final, kill was claimed during the fateful mission that saw Col Kearby shot down and killed

tetchy when quizzed by the press on his motivation to continually seek out combat sorties when effectively barred from such flying. He repeatedly stated that he was not out to break any record. 'I just like to hunt', he explained. 'It isn't that I like to kill anybody, but I do like to hunt. Since we are hunting in good, profitable ground, it makes each flight really a stimulant'.

By 23 December Neel Kearby had taken his score to 17 destroyed and one damaged in just under four months of combat. He had proven time and again that the Thunderbolt could do the job in the Pacific, and he went into the new year determined to eclipse Dick Bong's score and, perhaps more importantly, prove that the big Republic fighter was equally as effective as the Lightning.

No further P-47 aces were crowned within V FC until well into 1944, although P-38 ace Maj Jerry Johnson claimed two kills (his 11th and 12th victories) in December-January. These came soon after

Col Neel Kearby is presented with his Congressional Medal of Honor by the Commander of the Fifth Air Force, Gen George C Kenney, at the 348th FG's Finschhafen base in early 1944. A number of other P-47 pilots also received awards at this ceremony, including Kearby's replacement as head of the 348th FG, Lt Col Dick Rowland

his squadron (the famed 9th FS, nicknamed the 'Flying Knights') had transitioned to the more numerous Thunderbolt due to a shortage of Lightnings in-theatre in the wake of the large-scale air battles over Rabaul in October-November 1943.

The 'dyed-in-the-wool' P-38 pilots were less than impressed with the P-47D-4s that replaced their war-weary Lightnings, and this squadron proved to be the only one within the 49th FG to receive the Thunderbolt – the group's remaining two units persevered with their obsolescent P-40s until the 49th made a full conversion onto the P-38J in mid-1944.

Just to prove how unsuccessful the 9th FS was with the P-47 during it brief flirtation with the fighter, only two other aces within the unit aside from Johnson scored single kills whilst flying the 'Jug' – Capt Ralph Wandrey claimed his sixth, and last, victory (a 'Zeke') over Wewak on 13 March 1944, and Capt Wally Jordan downed an 'Oscar' over Boram (his second kill in a final tally of six) 24 hours later.

Despite its undistinguished spell with the 9th FS, the P-47 had long since proven its worth in the Southwest Pacific through the outstanding exploits of the 348th FG, and Col Neel Kearby in particular. Although the Thunderbolt's spell with the 'Flying Knights' had shown that it would never be a favourite amongst most P-38 veterans, even the most ardent defenders of the Lockheed fighter had a grudging respect for the P-47 by the end of 1943.

P-51s OVER BURMA

With other theatres both in the Pacific and Europe being deemed more important in the overall war effort in the eyes of senior Allied commanders, the China-Burma-India (CBI) front therefore consistently became one of the last to receive reinforcements (both in respect to men and machinery) throughout the conflict. Fortunately, Gen Claire Chennault, who headed the Allied air forces in China, was something of a tactical genius, and he quickly learned how to employ his few fighters to full effect in defence of his vast territories.

The first real sign of additional USAAF assets at last being available came in September 1943 when two groups equipped with P-40s joined the Tenth Air Force further south along the Burma front. Both outfits would subsequently enjoy greater logistical support than those units flying with the isolated Fourteenth Air Force in China.

Aside from the arrival of the two P-40 groups, the 311th Fighter-Bomber Group (FBG) also took up residence in this 'forgotten' theatre (at Nawadih, in India) during the same month, its 528th and 529th Fighter-Bomber Squadrons (FBS) flying A-36 Apache dive-bombers, whilst its 530th FBS was equipped with P-51A Mustangs. These examples of North American Aviation's future 'classic' were the first to see

Pilots of the 530th FBS/311th FBG pose in front of group commander Col Charles G Chandler's P-51A *KATHLEEN*. The group's ranking ace, James England, can be seen at the extreme left of the photo. Note that the pilot stood second from right is wearing an A-2 leather jacket adorned with a CBI theatre patch and 'Yellow Scorpions' logo – the latter was the nickname of the 530th FBS (*Carl Fischer*)

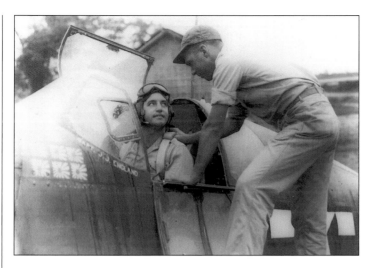

Capt England is wished 'happy hunting' by his crew chief at Dinjan in the spring of 1944. The former is almost certainly strapped into his ever-reliable P-51A-1 Mustang 43-6077 *Jackie*, which he used to down the bulk of his kills (*William Wolf*)

action against the Japanese, along with a small number that reached the 23rd FG at Kweilin, in China, at around the same time.

By the middle of 1944 all three squadrons within the 311th FG (redesignated in May of that year) had been equipped with later model P-51s, and would fight their way through Burma into China. By war's end, the original Mustang-equipped 530th FS and the P-38 Lightning-equipped 459th FS (see *Osprey Aircraft of the Aces 14 - P-38 Lightning Aces of the Pacific and CBI* for details) had provided the majority of the aces within the Tenth Air Force.

As previously mentioned, the 530th FBS were P-51A 'pioneers' when it came to fighting the Japanese over the jungles of Burma. The Mustang had, up that point in the war, seen limited action with the RAF on armed reconnaissance missions over northern Europe, and with the USAAF in the Mediterranean (see *Osprey Aircraft of the Aces 7 - P-51 Mustang Aces of the Ninth and Fifteenth Air Forces and the RAF* for details). As a result of these skirmishes, both air forces had severely criticised the performance of the fighter's Allison V-1710-81 at altitudes exceeding 15,000 ft. However, with the Japanese seeming to prefer to operate at well below this height, the marvellous design qualities of the P-51 came into their own in the CBI.

The 530th was initially stationed near Assam, on the northern India-Burma border, and soon after their arrival in-theatre, it was decided that the squadron would participate in a series of attacks on the Rangoon area commencing on 25 November 1943. The Mustangs were fitted with long-range fuel tanks and temporarily forward-based at Cox's Bazaar to serve as escorts for B-25 bombers sent to strike at the former RAF airfield at Mingaladon. The Japanese responded with a vigorous series of attacks by Ki-43 'Oscars' and Ki-45 'Nicks', and in the resulting melee, a single example of the latter twin-engined heavy fighter was destroyed and a second listed as 'probably shot down'. Two 'Oscars' were also 'probably shot down' as well, although two Mustangs were definitely lost and a further two badly damaged.

Two days later the P-51As joined P-38s of the 459th FS as escorts for formations of B-24s and B-25s again sent to attack targets in and around Rangoon. The medium bombers were assigned to strike at the Insein engine sheds, and were escorted by five 530th FBS aircraft, whilst the B-24s were escorted by ten Mustangs and arrived over their target at around 1330. 'Oscars' of the crack 64th Sentai and 'Nicks' of the 21st Sentai (see *Osprey Aircraft of the Aces 13 - Japanese Army Air Force Aces 1937-45* for details) offered spirited opposition, claiming two Mustangs, two Lightnings and three Liberators.

In return, the Mustangs shot down at least two 'Oscars' (three were reported as destroyed by the P-51 pilots, however), and also claimed

Another view of *Jackie*, England and his crew chief, taken some months earlier than the photo on the previous page (*William Wolf*)

additional fighters as probables or damaged whilst giving the bombers as effective protection as their limited numbers allowed. Future ten-kill ace Lt James England got his first confirmed 'Oscar' (he actually claimed a 'Zeke', with a second Mitsubishi fighter reportedly damaged) during this mission, having downed the single 'Nick' credited to the 530th FBS 48 hours earlier. Lt Bob Mulhollem went one better by being credited with the destruction of two 'Oscars' and a third as a probable. Having dominated the early skirmishes flown by the unit, both pilots would go on to become the first aces of the 530th FBS.

JAPANESE PERSPECTIVE

These first two actions had proven costly for the 311th FBG, resulting in four aircraft having been lost – including that flown by the group commander, Col Harry R Melton, Jr. It is believed that he fell victim to no less a pilot than veteran 64th Sentai ace, Lt Yohei Hinoki, in the first encounter between the two protagonists on 27 November 1943. The latter pilot had been scrambled with his flight in response to the incursion by the Mustang squadron, and when he visually acquired the USAAF fighters, he was unsure of their identity. Hinoki rocked the wings of his 'Oscar' in an attempt to ascertain its origins, and when Melton responded with a burst of fire, he quickly manoeuvred onto the tail of his less battle-experienced opponent and shot him down. Melton bailed out of his critically damaged Mustang and was soon captured.

Two days later Hinoki claimed yet another Mustang during the large-scale attack on Rangoon, plus a P-38 and a B-24 from the 308th Bomb Group (BG). Whilst closing on a second Liberator as the bombers departed the target area, the Japanese ace was in turn set upon by Bob Mulhollem, who all but shot Hinoki's 'Oscar' out of the air. The American's well-aimed fire shattered his opponent's right leg and shot up

The opposite side of *Jackie* reveals the unofficial emblem (a diving bird on a bomb) of the 530th FBS (*William Wolf*)

most of the Ki-43's airframe, but left the engine sufficiently intact for him to return to base. Hinoki somehow managed to evade Mulhollem's further attentions and limped home – it is almost certain that his 'Oscar' was the probable claimed by the American pilot in his mission report.

Hinoki subsequently had his right leg amputated, and upon recovery, was sent back to Japan. In the last desperate days of the war, Yohei Hinoki returned to active duty through the use of an artificial leg, and during the defence of the home islands, he claimed yet another Mustang on 16 July 1945 (a P-51D flown by Capt John W Benbow of the 457th FS/506th FG) whilst flying a Ki-100-I-Otsu *Goshikisen* of the Akeno Fighter School.

These early clashes with the P-51A left the Japanese indifferent to the fighting qualities of the aircraft. It seemed to them to be little more than a faster P-40, boasting less armament. The most feared opponent of the Japanese in the CBI at that time was the British Spitfire Mk VC, the first examples of which had arrived in India for the RAF just prior to the Mustang. Some Japanese pilots were so eager to engage, and beat, the much-vaunted Spitfire that many claimed victories over the Supermarine fighter during the raids on Rangoon in late November. None had actually participated in these actions, however.

Caught in reflective mood, Capt James John England contemplates his next sortie over the jungles of Burma in early 1944

FINAL RAIDS

On 1 December 1943 the last in the series of raids on Rangoon was made. Again, the Japanese responded vigorously, shooting down a number of B-24s. Three 'Oscars' were in turn claimed by the escorts, with the 530th FS claiming one of these for the similar loss of a single Mustang. Following this mission the 530th FBS returned east to the 311th FBG's base near Assam, where its rejoined the two A-36 units. As these accounts show, fortunes for the P-51 had initially been mixed, although the deployment ended on a positive note when the 530th intercepted an incoming Japanese bombing raid despatched in the aftermath of the mission to Rangoon on 1 December. Mustang pilots claimed two Ki-21 'Sally' bombers and an escorting 'Oscar' destroyed, as well as several more aircraft damaged, all for no loss.

Few actions of consequence then took place until March of 1944 when, on the 27th of that month, the P-51 enjoyed one of its best days with the Tenth Air Force. Eighteen Ki-49 'Helen' heavy bombers, escorted by 20 fighters (mostly 'Oscars'), made an assault on the airfields around Ledo, which prompted around 85 P-40s and P-51As to take off in their defence. Some 23 Allied fighters – including several Mustangs from the 311th FBG – succeeded in breaking through to the bombers, and they duly claimed nearly every Japanese 'Helen' as either destroyed or damaged.

This action, which took place in

Although of poor quality, this rare view shows 311th FG ace, Lt Bob Mulhollem, peering out of an open sliding canopy panel whilst sat in 'his' P-51A in mid-1944. All five of his kills were scored in Burma (*Steve Blake*)

the late morning east of India's North Pass, saw now-Capt James England enjoy his best day in combat when he claimed two 'Oscars' and a 'Helen' shot down, as well as a third 'Oscar' and a second 'Helen' damaged. This haul took his score to five, thus making him the first P-51 ace in the CBI. At least five other Japanese fighters and bombers were also credited to Mustang pilots.

Following this eventful day, the 311th FBG was again presented with little action over northern Burma primarily because they had inflicted such losses on the Japanese on 27 March. Indeed, it wasn't until the 530th FBS started conducting fighter sweeps over central Burma that Mustangs pilots could again begin to add to their scores.

During the first half of 1944, both the 459th (with its P-38s) and the 530th harassed and shot up numerous Japanese airfields, with the base at Meiktila coming in for special attention. April and May proved to be especially rewarding months, with many days of 'good hunting' being experienced by both American squadrons that resulted in large number of Japanese aircraft being claimed both in the air and on the ground.

Three May days in particular stand out for the 530th. On the 11th a sweep over Meiktila netted the P-51s at least ten Japanese aircraft, with Capt England claiming an 'Oscar' and a 'Tojo' (in P-51A-1 43-6077) to maintain his lead with seven confirmed victories.

Lt Mulhollem also shot down two fighters (which he claimed were Zeros, but were probably 'Oscars'), thus registering his third and fourth aerial kills in the process –he was also credited with damaging an 'Oscar' on the same sortie. Lt Ken Granger 'bagged' two Ki-43s as well, which he later followed up with four aircraft destroyed on the ground during his remaining time in Burma. Although the Tenth and Fourteenth Air Forces had authorised the recognition of ground claims in order to encourage aggressive action against enemy aircraft, they did not go as far

1st Air Commando Group (ACG) P-51As beat up their base at Broadway Strip, Burma, after completing an escort mission with their B-25 Mitchells, one of which had just landed. The 1st ACG was a composite outfit with their own fighters, bombers and transports, and due to its dedication to the close-air support mission, its Mustang pilots scored few kills. Indeed, the only ace to claim a victory whilst flying a 1st ACG P-51A was veteran pilot Lt Col Grant Mahony. He had claimed his previous four kills in P-40Es over the Philippines and Java during the first weeks of the Japanese invasion in late 1941 and early 1942, and had to wait until 17 April 1944 to get his all-important fifth kill flying a P-51A over Imphal (*Michael O'Leary*)

This P-47D was part of the 90th FS/80th FG based in India in 1944. No pilots were able to 'make ace' exclusively on Thunderbolts in the CBI, the individual who came closest to achieving this being Lt Sam Hammer of the 90th FS. He downed three 'Tojos' while flying a P-47 on 14 December 1944, and these combined with two kills (both 'Helen' bombers) scored nine months earlier in a P-40N to make him the 80th FG's sole ace (*W M Kampmeyer via J Crow*)

The only P-51As to see action against the Japanese were those flown exclusively by CBI-dedicated units, namely the 311th and 23rd FGs and the 1st ACG. The latter adopted these very distinctive five white stripes around the fuselages of their P-51As, this marking also being worn by its B-25s. Although operating in extremely rough conditions in the CBI, the Mustangs – and their Allison engines – proved to be up to the task. The lead aircraft in this 'two-ship' carries the name "*Mrs Virginia*" on its weathered nose – note the heavy exhaust staining along the length of the P-51A's fuselage, and that the forward portions of the spinners on both aircraft have been left in natural metal. Photographed near the Chin Hills, the second Mustang is being flown by 1st ACG CO, Col Phil Cochran, who became the character 'Flip Corkran' in the popular postwar American comic strip *Terry and the Pirates* (*Michael O'Leary*)

as the Eighth Air Force in England, which accorded these kills the same status as an aerial victory.

The next day more successes were scored over Meiktila as the 530th FS (redesignated that month) scored a further eight kills. One of those credited with a victory was Bob Mullhollem, who downed a 'Tojo' to give him his fifth confirmed kill and, of course, ace status. Lt Leonard 'Randy' Reeves also destroyed a 'Tojo' (and damaged a second) during the engagement, and he would later go on to score a further five kills in P-51s before his tour ended in September 1945.

Finally, the unit's ranking ground victory ace 'opened his account' by damaging a 'Tojo', Lt Bob Reed subsequently destroying two enemy aircraft in the air and 14 on the ground.

The final 'big' May day came on the 14th when a quartet of Japanese aircraft were added to the 530th FS's haul during a 22-Mustang raid on Meiktila – P-38s from the 459th FS covered the P-51s during the attack. Capt England got another 'Tojo' to take his tally to eight, whilst Lt Mulhollem could only claim his Ki-44 as 'probably destroyed'. These victories were the last to be scored by the Tenth Air Force's Mustang aces, and at the end of August 1944, the 311th FG was assigned to the Fourteenth Air Force in China. This left the little remaining air combat to be fought over Burma to the P-38s of the 459th FS.

END IN CHINA

A handful of further kills fell to the 530th FS following its move to Pungchacheng, in China, Maj James England (who was now CO of the squadron) taking his final score to ten by claiming a further two 'Oscars', with a third Ki-43 damaged, by year-end. Coinciding with the group's move to China was its re-equipment with P-51Cs, although the 311th FG had few chances to prove itself in aerial combat with the new fighter. The 530th scored the last of its wartime haul of 85 kills during two air battles in the Nanking area on 24/25 March 1945. Fittingly, four of these victories fell to the unit's only Fourteenth Air Force aces, Lt Lester Arasmith accounting for an 'Oscar' on the 24th (and a 'Tojo' damaged) to take his final score to six, and Lt Leonard Reeves destroying a 'Tojo' and a Ki-43 24 hours later – the latter pilot's final tally was also six.

FIFTH AIR FORCE P-47s IN 1944-45

By the beginning of 1944, Col Neel Kearby had almost realised both of his ambitions in the Southwest Pacific. The P-47 comprised almost half of V FC's overall frontline strength, and he had increased his tally of Japanese aircraft destroyed to 21 in the first nine days of the New Year.

The Thunderbolt's rise to numerical prominence in the Pacific had been accelerated by the loss of 16 precious P-38s (and the damaging of many others) during the massive November 1943 aerial assault on Rabaul. With few replacement Lockheed fighters available, and squadrons desperate to make good their losses, group commanders within the Fifth Air Force realised that they had little option but to accept the P-47.

This 'fate' befell the 9th and 39th FSs in late 1943, the veteran P-38 units effectively performing the unthinkable of just a few months earlier. The pilots of both units had great respect for the P-38, and despised the P-47. This feeling persisted throughout the conversion period, and surely had some bearing on the 39th failing to score a single confirmed kill until late 1944 – although also seeing little action, the 9th did actually account for the handful of enemy aircraft that ventured south to the Gusap area in the months that followed the P-47's arrival (see chapter one).

Maj Jerry 'Johnny Eager' Johnson command of the 9th FS during this period, and as previously mentioned, he quickly scored his first P-47 victory during a flight to the unit's new base at Gusap, about 100 miles north of the recently-conquered town of Lae, on 10 December 1943.

Wearing standard 348th FG markings, Lt Col Dick Rowland's *MISS MUTT II/ PRIDE OF LODI OHIO* is seen parked in its dispersal early in 1944 (*Krane Files*)

Whilst en route, the American pilots were vectored onto a large formation of Japanese fighters that were attempting to intercept USAAF transport aircraft. Quickly living up to his nickname, Johnson rushed headlong into the enemy formation and picked off a Ki-61 'Tony' as it was pressing home its attack on a defenceless C-47.

Fellow P-38 ace Capt Ralph Wandrey was also flying a P-47 within the formation when it was led into battle by Maj Johnson. Like most other pilots within the 9th FS, he was a Lightning man through and through, to the point where he claims to have called his P-47 flight members to attention whenever a P-38 flew over 'in reverence to a real airplane'. Although Wandrey had already scored five victories by 10 December, he missed out on a certain sixth kill on this day when a faulty gun switch on his P-47 rendered his armament useless. Years later, he recounted the action;

'The four of us began diving (in formation) on a bunch of Zeros strafing the field. But I kept my eye on 12 or 15 of them which were circling above us and looking us over. The strafers scattered as we dove into them, and we picked a group of six off to one side as our targets. The one I aimed at began climbing, and as I tried to follow him I found that my plane wouldn't pull out of the dive – my elevator control was jammed. My airspeed registered over 400, and I had only enough time to roll my plane on its side and kick the top rudder with all I had . . .

'When I joined the other three boys (after recovering), I saw a Zero climbing up from below me. He zoomed up and rolled over on his back about 70 yards ahead of me – directly in my gunsight. I was pressing the trigger frantically before I realised nothing was happening. I checked all my switches to make certain they were on – and still my guns wouldn't shoot. As my target started to dive toward the ground, I gave my plane full throttle and dove at the Zero's tail. I felt a sharp bump as I passed through his prop wash and knew I missed him and had better get to the field below me.'

Wandrey did, however, eventually score a victory in the P-47 when he claimed a 'Zeke' near the Japanese base at Wewak during a raid on 13 March 1944. The very next day, the 9th FS's sole remaining ace to score a kill in the P-47 claimed his solitary victory. Capt Wallace Jordan had enjoyed just a single success with the P-38H-1 (as early as 2 August 1943), and had had to wait until 14 March 1944 to double his score, when he

Top and above
P-47D-3 *DARING DOTTIE III* was assigned to 341st FS CO, Capt John Moore. The eagle-eyed amongst you will have noticed that the aircraft's finish differs In these two photos, both of which were taken in early 1944. In the top shot, the P-47's rear fuselage has been stripped of paint, whilst in the lower photo, the Thunderbolt has no exposed areas. This suggests that the finish was more of an experiment scheme, pending the switch to unpainted aircraft from March 1944 onwards (*W Hess*)

Maj Jerry Johnson's P-47D-4 is seen almost certainly in January 1944. The taped off area beneath the cockpit will soon feature 11 Japanese flags, denoting his tally up to that point in the war (*Krane files*)

The diminutive Capt Johnson (far right) signs off his flight log at either Dobodura or Nadzab in early 1944 (*Ferguson*)

claimed a Ki-43 over Boram. Later nicknamed 'Major Stitch' after suffering a head wound in a jeep accident on base, Jordan would score a further four kills in P-38Ls before year-end.

Despite enjoying virtually all his successes with the Lightning, 'Wally' Jordan considered the armament of the P-47 to be better than that fitted to the P-38 for fighter-versus-fighter combat. He also claimed that the Thunderbolt was the more manoeuvrable of the two aircraft at a higher altitude. In general, he seemed to conclude that the P-47 was well suited to combat against Japanese fighter, while the P-38 was more effective against bombers.

Some weeks prior to Wandrey and Jordan scoring their respective kills with the P-47, their CO, Maj Johnson, had claimed his second confirmed P-47 victory (and 11th kill out of a final tally of 22) during a late-morning high-altitude sweep of the Wewak area by 15 9th FS aircraft on 18 January 1944. The following extract from Johnson's combat report records his impressions of the subsequent engagement, which saw him come to the aid of a fellow P-47 pilot who found himself under attack from above;

'I turned into the Japanese fighter (a 'Zeke') and followed him in a dive toward Wewak. I fired a long burst from dead astern. I closed to about 50 yards and fired from the dead astern position. There were several bright flashes as my fire hit his left wing root, fuselage and tail. He twisted to the left, diving straight into the jungle, smoking and apparently out of control. I was diving at 500 miles an hour and started pulling out at 5000 ft.'

Despite his double success with the Thunderbolt, Johnson was totally convinced of the superiority of the P-38 over the P-47, and reputedly agreed to challenge Neel Kearby to a mock combat to determine the relative merits of each type. Although the contest apparently never materialised, Johnson's ability

to dogfight in the Lightning was reputedly proven later in the war when he 'bested' a P-51D to the point where he followed his opponent through every attempted evasive manoeuvre with one of the P-38's engines shut down!

DEATH OF NEEL KEARBY

During the first few months of 1944, the leading aces in the Pacific became fixated with the challenge of becoming the first American pilot to better ranking World War 1 ace Eddie Rickenbacker's almost myth-

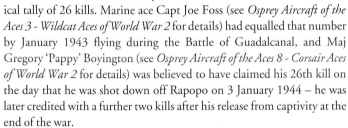

ical tally of 26 kills. Marine ace Capt Joe Foss (see *Osprey Aircraft of the Aces 3 - Wildcat Aces of World War 2* for details) had equalled that number by January 1943 flying during the Battle of Guadalcanal, and Maj Gregory 'Pappy' Boyington (see *Osprey Aircraft of the Aces 8 - Corsair Aces of World War 2* for details) was believed to have claimed his 26th kill on the day that he was shot down off Rapopo on 3 January 1944 – he was later credited with a further two kills after his release from captivity at the end of the war.

The top USAAF ace in January 1944 was Capt Richard Bong, who had taken his tally to 21 confirmed kills by the end of the Rabaul sweeps on 5 November 1943. Sent on 60 days leave less than a week later, he had to wait until 15 February 1944 to claim his 22nd victory, which took the form of a 'Tony' over New Britain. Bong usually flew with his friend, and mentor, Tommy Lynch, who had himself scored his 17th kill on 10 February.

Neel Kearby had not added to his score of 21 by the end of January, and he was growing increasingly impatient at his prospects of bettering the Rickenbacker record due to the decreased levels of activity in his main 'hunting ground' over Wewak. Other concerns also played on his mind, for he knew that the P-47's days of dominance in New Guinea would not last forever. With production of new-model P-38s at last starting to catch up with USAAF demand, Kearby could see that the many Lightning aces within the Fifth Air Force would not be denied their sorely missed Lockheed fighters for much longer. Indeed, Gen Kenney had been soliciting his superiors for ample numbers to be committed to the Pacific since the beginning of the year. It was also only a matter of time before examples of the Packard Merlin-engined P-51 became available in sufficient numbers to largely replace the P-47.

Kearby realised that the only way he could save his beloved Thunderbolt from swift retirement in the Southwest Pacific was to break Rickenbacker's record. He reasoned that the resulting publicity from such an achievement would surely secure the P-47's future until war's end. He was also conscious of the personal glory associated with beating the 26-year-old record score for an American pilot.

Many of Kearby's peers considered him to be the consummate fighter

Top and above
The 9th FS's Lt Ralph Wandrey is seen both in and out of the cockpit prior to scoring his one and only kill in the P-47. A devotee of the P-38, Wandrey harbored no real affection for the Thunderbolt, dubbing his own fighter *REPUBLIC'S ABORTION*! However, he did confirm one Japanese fighter over Wewak on 13 March 1944 when he found himself all alone over a formation of several enemy fighters. Having shot down his victim (a 'Zeke'), Wandrey used the P-47's unrivalled ability to dive at speed to effect his escape from Wewak at low level (*Krane Files*)

pilot, easily capable of passing the Rickenbacker score. However, his goal was now being seriously challenged by both Dick Bong and Tommy Lynch, who were enjoying renewed success flying together on specially arranged missions deep into enemy territory. Kearby knew that just one such sortie could push either of them past the 26 mark within weeks or even days.

On the morning of 5 March 1944 both Bong and Lynch were credited with two kills apiece whilst attacking Tadji airfield, these successes raising the former's score to 24 victories and the latter's to 19. Hearing of his great rivals' success, and sensing that the historic moment seemed to be at hand, Kearby felt the need to quickly add to his score. Twenty-four hours later, he hastily organised a freelance fighter sweep again to Tadji with his two old friends 'Dinghy' Dunham and Sam Blair. Short of the intended target, Kearby instead led his flight along the familiar coastal patrol line near Wewak at a height of 22,000 ft.

A 'Tony' was soon sighted approaching the Dagua strip, but Kearby quickly realised that the Ki-61 would be safely on the ground before it could be intercepted, so he decided not to attack. Less than five minutes later his patience was seemingly rewarded when three bombers (misidentified at the time as G3M 'Nells', they were almost certainly Ki-48 'Lilys' of the 75th Sentai) were sighted at just 500 ft above the sea, heading for Dagua strip. The trio of American pilots immediately attacked.

Owing to sufficient surprise and superior height, Dunham and Blair quickly shot down their targets. However, Kearby's victim was anything but a certain claim, and he decided to make a complete circle to attack again. By performing such a manoeuvre, he violated two of his own cardinal rules – never lose speed or altitude whilst engaged in combat.

Although Kearby soon made quick work of the bomber, he had lost all his height and speed ensuring its destruction, and he now found himself 'low and slow' – a deadly combination in the big Thunderbolt. He was swiftly attacked from above by a solitary Ki-43 from the veteran 77th Sentai, the pilot being able to draw close enough to the wallowing P-47 in order to fire a burst of heavy calibre 12.7 mm rounds into the cockpit before an aroused Capt Dunham got into range and belatedly shot the 'Oscar' off Kearby's tail (this took 'Dinghy's' tally to nine).

With the unexpected fighter threat neutralised, Dunham and Blair searched diligently for Kearby but soon ran short of fuel and had to return to base. Upon landing at Saidor, the former pilot was so distraught at the loss of his friend that he insisted on immediately returning to the area in another P-47 to search for his comrade. In the end, Dunham had to be physically restrained from taking off by his fellow pilots.

Neel Kearby was to remain missing in action until the autumn of 1948 when, after a lengthy investigation by the War Graves Commission, it was agreed that the remains of a USAAF pilot found by Australian War Graves personnel in March 1946 were indeed those of

Neel Kearby poses with one of his familiarly-named Thunderbolts in early 1944. Note the star design on the aircraft's wheel cover behind him. Most of the senior officers within the 348th FG used personal designs on the mainwheels of their respective P-47s, Lt Col Rowland, for example, using the 'five in a comet' motif from the Fifth Air Force badge

Fiery Ginger III runs up prior to taxying out on a sortie. Kearby had scored at least 12 victories confirmed by the time he turned this veteran P-47D over to the 58th FG in early 1944. Pilots of the latter group thought it somewhat odd that such a venerable fighter should end its days flying routine ground attack missions

the Fifth Air Force's ranking P-47 ace. His remains were flown back to his beloved Texas for burial on 16 June 1949.

By interviewing numerous local villagers in the Magahen area of northern New Guinea soon after the discovery of the body, it was learned that Col Kearby had succeeded in bailing out of his stricken P-47D-4 (42-22668). However, he had subsequently died from bullet wounds inflicted by the 'Oscar' pilot when his parachute snagged in the dense jungle canopy.

The Japanese bomber that Neel Kearby attacked had brought him his 22nd, and last, victory.

FINAL KILLS IN NEW GUINEA

Whilst most groups that converted onto the P-47 in late 1943 had come to the Thunderbolt from the Lightning, the 35th FG received its first Republic fighters in January 1944 as replacements for both the Lockheed 'twin' and a clutch of decidedly obsolescent P-39 and P-400 Airacobras. Two of the group's three squadrons (the 40th and 41st FSs) had been flying the venerable Bell fighter in combat for two years, whilst its remaining unit, the 39th FS, had been P-38-equipped since November 1942.

The first 35th FG pilot to attain ace status following the arrival of the P-47 was Maj William McDonough, who had already scored two kills and a probable with the P-39K whilst flying with the 40th FS in February 1943. Posted to group HQ later that year, he nevertheless continued to participate in operations with his old unit whenever the opportunity arose, and on 15 February 1944 he downed a 'Zeke' and an 'Oscar' over Wewak. 'Mac' McDonough achieved his fifth kill (a Ki-61) on 4 March near Gusap, after which he was transferred to V FC HQ. He was subsequently killed in a flying accident on 22 April 1944 whilst awaiting transportation home.

Further P-47 successes also came to the 40th and 41st FSs in March, with a single pilot from each unit attaining 'acedom' during fighter sweeps over the Wewak area on the 11th and 13th that saw the Thunderbolt credited with almost 30 Japanese aircraft destroyed.

Like 'Mac' McDonough, Capt Bob Yaeger had also enjoyed success with the Airacobra whilst serving with the 40th FS in 1943, scoring a brace of kills on 15 August in P-39N-5 42-19012. He went one

Below and bottom
Fiery Ginger IV is seen in January 1944, with one scoreboard showing 21 kills and the other 22 – the latter shot fuels the notion that Kearby was not flying his own P-47 on the mission that saw him killed. However, the constructor's number 419 on the fuselage side clearly coincides with P-47D-4 serial 42-22668. If only the photographer of the latter photo could have sighted himself a bit more to the right so that the serial on the aircraft's tail was visible!

HOYT'S HOSS was the mount of Capt Edward P Hoyt of the 41st FS, who managed to claim four 'Oscars' in March 1944. He finally achieved his fifth victory on 13 August 1945 when he returned to combat in a P-47N with the 465th FS

better on 11 March 1944 when he downed two 'Tonys' and an 'Oscar' near Wewak. Two days later Capt Francis Dubisher 'made ace' when he downed an 'Oscar' over the Dagua strip area, near Wewak, whilst flying a P-47D-11. Having claimed four confirmed victories in two actions with the Bell fighter in 1943, the 41st FS pilot had had to endure a seventh-month wait before scoring his fifth, and final, victory.

For squadronmate Lt Edward Hoyt, seven months must have seemed a very short time indeed, for after scoring four 'Oscar' kills in a successful bout of action between 11 and 14 March, he would not get his fifth victory in the P-47 until 13 August 1945! By then he had transferred to the 465th FS/507th FG, based on Ie Shima, and was flying Very-Long-Range (VLR) bomber escort missions in P-47Ns over great swathes of Japan and Korea. Hoyt's final victory was over a 'Betty' bomber off the coast of the latter country, and it proved to be one of the last Allied aerial kills of the war.

Whilst the P-47 'novices' of the 35th FG enjoyed their first successes with the aircraft, the Thunderbolt veterans of the 348th FG continued to prove their undoubted mastery of the big fighter by taking a heavy toll of the enemy during the same March engagements. On the 11th 14 Japanese fighters fell to P-47D-11s of the 340th FS during a sweep of Wewak, with one of the successful pilots on this occasion being Lt Myron Hnatio. His single 'Zeke' (almost certainly an 'Oscar') kill took his final wartime tally to exactly five, and in his combat report the newly-crowned ace described the critical moment in the sortie with understated brevity;

'. . . came in dead astern firing all the way. He started smoking, rolled over and crashed into the sea two miles offshore, opposite But airdrome.'

Squadronmate Lt Michael Dikovitsky also claimed a fighter (correctly identified as an 'Oscar') during the Wewak sortie, taking his tally to three. He had achieved his success by pulling enough lead on the twisting and turning fighter to fire off a 60° deflection shot that sent it falling into the sea. Dikovitsky finally 'made ace' in December, when he destroyed single 'Zekes' on the 11th and the 22nd.

Lt Richard Fleischer also enjoyed success over Wewak on 11 March, downing a pair of 'Oscars' to add to his three previous kills from earlier in his tour. Having intercepted the Ki-43s with the rest of his unit, he made a head-on pass at one of the fighters and was startled to see the pilot jump to his death. Fleischer's second kill came when his opponent 'snapped to the left in a half roll and crashed into the water west of Kairiru Island'.

Future 342nd FS five-kill ace Lt Bob Sutcliffe scored his fourth victory (an 'Oscar') over Wewak on 19 March, and then demonstrated the necessary prudence often shown by the successful fighter pilot to return home and make his report, which included the following remarks;

'No evasive action was taken on my first pass, but the three ships executed a well planned manoeuvre on the second pass. The leader pulled

up into a tight loop, and the wingmen began tight "chandelles" to the right and left respectively. I saw what was coming and did not attempt to follow. Had I followed any one of the three, both of the other two would have been in excellent position to catch me in a cross-fire. This manoeuvre is a very tempting trap.'

Sutcliffe's cautiousness paid off eight days later when he safely claimed his fifth victory whilst on a patrol over the invasion beaches of Biak. He dived with his formation from 6000 ft onto a group of four 'Oscars' spotted some 5000 ft below them. The pilot of the Ki-43 that he destroyed probably never even saw the Thunderbolt that made the head-on pass which resulted in the Japanese fighter crashing into the trees a few miles east of Bosneck, on Biak Island.

The 348th FG enjoyed yet another 'purple patch' between 3 and 12 June when they claimed 18 Japanese aircraft shot down. The 342nd FS's Lt Marvin Grant was the stand-out pilot during this period, scoring four kills in two engagements, and thus taking his final tally to seven. His first successes came on the 4th when he encountered a flight of 'Oscars' whilst patrolling over a convoy near Bosneck. Three of the Ki-43s managed to roll and dive away, but Grant succeeded in firing an accurate 60° deflection burst into the fourth fighter, setting it on fire.

With one 'Oscar' destroyed, Grant quickly turned his attention to the wingman of his first victim, who was flying straight at him. Barely having time to take aim, the P-47 pilot shot off a quick burst at the rapidly closing Ki-43 before taking evasive action. Grant's rounds struck home with clinical accuracy, and his second victim crashed into the sea. Incensed by the loss of their comrades, several other 'Oscars' latched onto the tail of Grant's big fighter and chased him for about five minutes before he escaped and headed for home to report his fourth and fifth aerial victories (which he described in his paperwork as 'Zekes').

Capt Ed Roddy's crew chief poses on the wing the former's P-47D-2 in the spring of 1944. Roddy got his last confirmed victory when he down a 'Helen' bomber near the Japanese airbase at Borum on 4 February 1944. After leaving the 348th FG, he went on to command the 58th FG in 1945

Lt Bob Sutcliffe of the 342nd FS claimed his fifth aerial victory when he downed an 'Oscar' near Biak Island on 27 May 1944 (*Marshall Vickers*)

Eight days later, the 342nd FS had two aces crowned when both Marvin Grant and Capt Edward Popek scored multiple kills whilst on yet another convoy patrol off Biak Island. Two elements of P-47Ds intercepted a formation of five Imperial Navy B5N 'Kate' torpedo bombers, and quickly despatched them all with little fuss. Popek claimed three destroyed to add to his score of two from 1943, whilst Grant, who was leading the second element, accounted for the remaining two 'Kates' – all five were reported to have burst into flames as soon as they were hit by the Thunderbolts' initial shots.

BALIKPAPAN

By mid-1944, the deliberate Allied policy to cut off all supply routes to the large Japanese force in New Guinea had really started to have an effect. Few army or navy aircraft remained serviceable in-theatre, and those lost in combat were no longer being replaced by new stocks from Japan. With no enemy to fight, the number of Thunderbolts based in New Guinea with the Fifth Air Force also began to wane. They had secured the hotly-disputed zones along the north coast, and any long-distance pockets of resistance that still remained were allocated to the recently arrived P-38J, which was capable of performing both the escort and dive-bombing missions in a single sortie.

There was, however, one last target in New Guinea that every available P-38 and P-47 would be needed for. Since overrunning the Dutch East Indies in the early weeks of the war, the Japanese had been taking advantage of the region's oil resources through the huge refinery

A flight of 39th FS P-47Ds cruises over northern New Guinea in the latter half of 1944. Aircraft '10' was usually flown by the squadron commander, and was almost certainly used by future eight-kill ace Lt LeRoy Grossheusch during this period

P-47D-2 42-27886 *Sylvia/Racine Belle* was the mount of 342nd FS ace Lt Marvin Grant. The scoreboard neatly painted on his aircraft shows all seven of his victories, which had been scored by the middle of June 1944. The Thunderbolt was photographed during the Philippines campaign of late 1944

at Balikpapan, on the island of Borneo. Indeed, the whole Japanese 'war machine' had been effectively sustained through the exploitation of these petroleum resources. Despite its importance to the enemy, the refinery had only been attacked by the Allies very occasionally due to its distance from USAAF and RAF bases. However, with the containment of Japanese opposition in New Guinea, and new strategic gains in the north-west of the country, there was now an opportunity to mount a series of large-scale escorted raids.

On 10 October 1944 the first such mission to Balikpapan took place, with Fifth and Thirteenth Air Force B-24s (see *Osprey Combat Aircraft 11 - B-24 Liberator Units of the Pacific War* for details) operating from the recently captured island of Noemfoor, escorted by P-47D-28s from the 35th FG and P-38Ls from the 49th.

Former Airacobra pilot Lt William 'Wild Bill' Strand of the 40th FS proved to be the 'star of the day' when he downed three 'Oscars' over Borneo. Forty-eight hours later he destroyed a further two Ki-43s directly over the refinery complex during the second mission to Balikpapan, this double haul taking his score to six destroyed, one probable and one damaged (all these successes were against 'Oscars', with a single kill and the probable being scored in November 1943 in a P-39N-5).

Another former Airacobra pilot tasting success for the first time since late 1943 was Capt Alvaro Hunter, who had downed two 'Oscars' over north-eastern New Guinea in a 40th FS P-39Q almost a year earlier. He repeated this feat on 14 October by again destroying two Ki-43s, this time over Balikpapan. Hunter finally achieved 'acedom' on 24 November when he claimed yet another 'Oscar' whilst participating in the early fighter sweeps of the Philippines – he was CO of the 40th FS by this late stage in his combat tour.

Not all pilots that tasted victory on the 14th were 'old hands', for future six-kill ace Lt James Mugavero of the 41st FS downed his first two victories – 'Oscars' – over Balikpapan's local airfield at Manggar.

Although the capture of Noemfoor Island had at last brought Balikpapan within range of USAAF escort fighters, the distances involved were still considerable, and used every last ounce of fuel that could be squeezed into the internal and external tanks of the P-38 and P-47. These raids also saw pilots reaping the benefits of the tuition given to them by America's greatest ever long-distance aviator, Charles Lindbergh. He had spent several months in-theatre with various groups during the summer of 1944 instructing pilots on the best methods of cruise control, which effectively added many miles to both fighter types, and made the Balikpapan missions possible.

Lindbergh's techniques involved very lean fuel mixes and strict control of the throttle, and although they gave the fighters the 'legs' required in the Southwest Pacific,

Lt Robert Knapp, also of the 342nd FS, poses on the wing of his P-47D-21 sometime between June and December 1944

they brought with them huge maintenance headaches for the long-suffering groundcrews. The latter were left to deal with engines that had been run on too thin a fuel mix for hours on end, resulting in all sorts of damage being inflicted on the carburettors and fuel injection systems.

THE PHILIPPINES

Gen Douglas MacArthur's long-awaited return to the Philippines became a reality on 20 October 1944 when American forces landed on Leyte. Several days later, the Fifth Air Force sent in fighters to the island's Tacloban airstrip, and thus established a permanent presence in the region.

The first victory scored by a P-47 ace was a 'Kate' claimed on 1 November by James Mugavero near the Island of Cebu, which boosted his overall tally to three. He only had to wait a further four days to score his fourth kill, which took the form of a 'Tony' intercepted off Negros Island.

The 348th FG was also an early arrival at Tacloban, this group now consisting of no fewer than four squadrons following the formation of the 460th FS in July 1944. Veteran Thunderbolt pilot, and ex-342nd FS boss, Capt 'Dinghy' Dunham, was put in command of the new squadron, and by the time he led his unit into the Philippines in November 1944, he had been promoted to major. Fittingly, Dunham became the first 348th FG ace to score a kill whilst flying from Tacloban when he downed a 'Zeke' Model 32 on 18 November;

'At 0740/I, while flying south over Ormoc at 10,000 ft, we were attacked by two enemy planes – a "Zeke 32" and an "Oscar". They dived from the west, and from an altitude of about 13,000 ft. We turned into them for a head-on pass, but they broke and started west toward Cebu. We climbed to pursue.

'I closed, firing from astern to within 30 yards of the "Zeke 32", which was hit many times in the fuselage and wings. It went into a straight dive and crashed into the water west of the Camotes Islands.'

When 'Dinghy' Dunham was given the job of establishing the all-new 460th FS, his task was made a little easier by the drafting in of a handful of seasoned pilots from the three established squadrons within the 348th FG. One of those individuals that made the swap was Lt George Della, who had been in-theatre with the 341st FS since August 1943, and had claimed a solitary kill (a Ki-61) four months later on 1 December.

Following his CO's lead, Della doubled his own score 24 hours after Denham had claimed the unit's opening victory of the campaign when he destroyed a 'Zeke' 32 near Cebu. Five days later Della 'bagged' a solitary J2M 'Jack', and then went looking for a second victim;

'I then joined in pursuit of a single remaining "Jack 11" toward Cebu.

This 342nd FS P-47D-21 was the mount of seven-kill ace Capt Ed Popek, seen here flanked by his dedicated groundcrew of Linden Kipps (left) and R H Franzen (right)

Lt Mike Dikovitsky of the 340th FS used this P-47D-23 (42-27899), which he christend *JOSIE/Cleveland Clever*, to down his final two (of five) kills in December 1944

Both (P-47s) and (P-38s) participated, but were unable to close sufficiently on the "Jack 11" to attack, gas supply, in my case, being low . . . The enemy pilot appeared aggressive, but unwilling to engage in combat.'

The third anniversary of the Pearl Harbor raid proved to be one of the great days for the Philippine air war, as swarms of Japanese aircraft attempted to repel the Allied landings taking place in Leyte's Ormoc Bay. The Fifth Air Force responded vigorously, accounting for more than 50 enemy aircraft – 12 of which were credited to P-47s of the 348th FG, which had only arrived on Leyte on 16 November.

'Dinghy' Dunham proved to be the most successful P-47 pilot on the day, claiming four kills during an afternoon patrol in which he led ten P-47s of the 460th on a sweep of San Isidoro Bay, which surrounds the island of Cebu, in the Camotes Sea. The American pilots ran into a formation of 15 'Zeke' 32s during the fighter sweep, and on their initial pass, Dunham shot up one of the A6Ms so badly that the pilot elected to bail out. He then sent a second fighter flaming into the sea before the enemy dispersed.

Forming up his squadron and continuing on with the patrol for a further 15 minutes, the major then spotted a formation of 'Oscars' and led the attack into the army fighters. Dunham once again swiftly despatched two of their number, thus beating the veteran ace's previous best tally of three kills in a sortie (three 'Vals' scored on 21 December 1943). His score now stood at 14.

7 December also saw the 341st FS register its first kill over the Philippines when veteran pilot Capt William Foulis downed a Ki-46 'Dinah' over Calangaman Island. This kill represented his second victory of the tour, for he had destroyed a solitary 'Zeke' on 27 December 1943. By Christmas Day 1944 Foulis's tally had risen to six.

Exactly a week later, the Fifth Air Force's P-47 units enjoyed yet another 'stellar day' when Thunderbolts of the 35th and 348th FGs accounted for no fewer than 20 of 21 Japanese aircraft claimed that day. Bill Dunham was again at the heart of the action, catching a pair of 'Sally' (or possibly 'Helen') bombers during an early-morning sweep of the Negros Island area. Surprising the vulnerable twin-engined aircraft, 'Dinghy' soon proved why he was the group's leading surviving ace by clinically despatching one of the Ki-21s, and so recording his 15th – and final – victory with the P-47.

Maj Bill Banks climbs out of his 348th FG HQ Flight P-47D-23 in late 1944. The nine-kill ace was a true egalitarian, who promised that no one would demote his crew chief other than himself, then went ahead and busted the sergeant! The two of them remained good friends until Banks passed away in 1983

Later that morning fellow squadron boss, Capt Meade Brown, was leading a flight of 340th FS P-47s again near Negros when he encountered a lone Ki-61 'Tony', which duly became the fourth of his eventual five victories. A member of the squadron since November 1942, Brown had claimed three kills and a probable in December 1943, but had then had to wait three days short of a full year to achieve 'acedom'. He would later lose his life in combat flying an F-51D with the 40th FIS/35th FG over Korea on 24 August 1950.

Returning to the 40th FS/35th FG of the Pacific War, one of the rising stars of the group was Lt Ellis Baker, who had claimed his first kill on 24 November 1944, and then added two more on 14 December south of Negros Island;

'I was flying No 2 position in "Frisco Red flight". The first flight of enemy bombers ("Helens") was sighted at 0940/I, slightly south of Soledad, at 9 o'clock on the deck from us.

'We attacked at once, the element leader taking the first flight, and "Red flight" leader and myself taking the second. Lt Steffy, "Red flight" leader, attacked the outside bombers of the second flight, firing a long burst from 45°. I observed hits in the engines, fuselage and wing roots. The plane crashed into the water and burst into flames.

'I attacked the inside bomber, firing a long burst from dead astern. I observed hits which set both motors afire. The bomber crashed into the water and burst into flames.

' I then pulled up to the left and made a gentle turn to the right. When I rolled out, I was flying on the left wing of another bomber. I slid in behind the bomber for a stern shot. The bomber helped me in this capacity by making a turn to the right. As the bomber rolled out of its turn, it put me in a position for a stern shot. I fired several long bursts and observed hits in the tail turret, both engines and parts of the fuselage. The bomber began smoking and started a steep dive, and immediately thereafter exploded in mid-air, resulting in slight damage to my plane as it passed over me.'

Perhaps the last great day for the 348th FG in World War 2 came on Christmas Eve, when the group escorted bombers sent to attack Clark Field, near Manila. Once over the target, the P-47 pilots fought an aggressive Japanese fighter defence, claiming more than 30 victories for the loss of just three of their own.

The 341st FS's Bill Foulis proved to be the 'star of the day' when he claimed three 'Oscars' destroyed and a fourth as a probable in a lively battle over the former USAAC base. This action commenced soon after 15 Ki-43s were spotted above and to the west of the raiding American force as they neared the target. Foulis was flight leader for the 341st FS contingent on this mission, and upon sighting the 'Oscars', he ordered his formation to immediately jettison their external tanks and climb up to engage the enemy.

Within minutes Foulis had downed a Ki-43 with a 30° deflection shot, then pulled head-on into the path of another 'Oscar'. The latter aircraft visibly fell apart under the sheer weight of fire from the attacking P-47 D-23, suffering hits to its engine and fuselage, before falling in flames to the ground. Foulis then pulled in behind a third Ki-43, which he also shot up, but could only claim as a probable for he did not see it crash. Finally, he had just enough ammunition left to take on a fourth 'Oscar' in yet another head-on pass, which inevitably resulted in destruction for the Nakajima fighter.

A further three P-47 aces also added two kills apiece to their respective scores on this day. Former 342nd FS boss Maj Bill Banks, who was now part of the 348th FG's flying staff, claimed a pair of 'Zekes' (plus a third damaged) to take his final wartime tally to nine – he had 'made ace' as long ago as 20 December 1943. Lt George Della, on the other hand, actually took his score to five with his double 'Zeke' haul, thus becoming the 460th FS's second, and last, ace. Finally, veteran 342nd FS pilot Lt George Davis claimed his last successes of World War 2 with yet another pair of 'Zekes' destroyed near Clark Field, increasing his tally to seven.

Davis, an aggressive West Texan from the town of Lubbock, seemed to exude pride in both his unit and his P-47, as evinced by his combat report for this sortie. He had already despatched one 'Zeke' with three shorts bursts from a deflection angle of a full 90° when he returned to cover the bombers and sighted another Mitsubishi fighter above him;

This 'bubble-top' P-47D of the 35th FG was photographed prior to a squadron number being applied. Note the Lockheed P-38-type drop tanks that also worked so well with the P-47

'... before he could make a pass at the bombers, I closed in from astern and fired at him from about 200 yards with no deflection. Some pieces flew off, and he then burst into flames and started down in a spin. My number three man saw this one crash. We then returned to the bombers and stayed with them until our fuel supply ran so low we were forced to leave them. I believe that up to the time we left the B-24s, no enemy fighters had gotten within firing range of them, although 10 to 15 aerial bombs had been dropped.'

Seven years later, during the Korean War, now Maj George Davis (CO of the F-86E-equipped 334th FIS/4th FIW) would be killed in action fighting MiG-15s over the Yalu River – but not before he had accounted for 14 MiGs, and posthumously won the Congressional Medal of Honor – see *Osprey Aircraft of the Aces 4 - Korean War* for details.

Lt Jim Mugavero poses in his 41st FS P-47D-28 *"Pitter Pat"*. He had scored four victories in this Thunderbolt during October and November 1944, and went on to claim his last two kills on a sweep south of Formosa on 31 January 1945

───────── **FINAL P-47 VICTORIES** ─────────

In the early months of 1945 both the 348th and 35th FGs commenced the transition onto the P-51D Mustang, and by the end of March the former group had flown its first operations with the North American Aviation fighter – the 35th FG completed its first missions just a few weeks later. That left just the ground-attack optimised 58th FG operating the P-47 within the Fifth Air Force, and this group remained loyal to the Thunderbolt until war's end.

Despite losing their beloved Republic fighter by the early spring, pilots (including a few aces) from both the 348th and 35th FGs still achieved a small number of kills in the first three months of 1945.

One such individual was Capt LeRoy Grossheusch, who had risen through the ranks of the 39th FS during 1944 to the point where he was made commander of the unit in November of that year. Soon after being

Maj 'Dinghy' Dunham's distinctively-marked P-47D-23 *Bonnie* (42-27884) is seen in the Philippines in mid December 1944 carrying kill markings for all 15 of its pilots successes with the Thunderbolt. This aircraft was arguably the most colourful fighter within the 460th FS, and was a suitable mount for the unit commander

made the 'boss', he scored his first victory (on 21 November) when he caught a lone Ki-46 'Dinah' reconnaissance aircraft flying over the island of Negros.

In late January 1945 the P-47 groups enjoyed a particularly successful period of aerial action, and LeRoy Grossheusch was one of those that took full advantage of the one-sided combats then taking place. On the 30th he downed two unidentified Japanese biplanes whilst on a sweep over Formosa, and he followed this up 11 days later with yet another pair of 'biplane trainers' and a 'Dinah' when he returned to same area.

The newly-crowned ace added a third Ki-46 (and his last kill with the P-47) to his growing tally on 25 February, this victory being rather unusual in that the 'Dinah' crashed into the sea *after* sunset – thus perhaps qualifying Capt Grossheusch as the first (and only?) pilot to score a night victory in the P-47. He had been leading a flight of four P-47s on a sweep over Formosa when two Ki-46s were sighted and intercepted in the area of Chikunan. Grossheusch's target took some hits from a 10° deflection shot, and its right engine was trailing flame as it fled into a cloud.

With his wingman staying close behind, Grossheusch followed his target into the cloud and then back out again into clearer skies, its engine still burning and trailing bits of debris. A further burst from the P-47's guns also started a fire in the left engine, and the Americans observed a crew member jump from the 'Dinah'. Finally, with the aircraft virtually engulfed in flames, the Ki-46 crashed violently into the sea below in the descending darkness at around 1815.

LeRoy Grossheusch's final kill came in a P-51D on 12 August when he tangled with a more fitting opponent in the shape of a Ki-84 'Frank' fighter. Its destruction took his final score to eight.

Returning to 30 January, the previously-mentioned Lt Ellis Baker of the 40th FS/35th FG also claimed a kill during a nine-ship sweep of Formosa. He was flying in the tail-end position of 'Frisco Red flight' in his P-47D-28 when he sighted and called out a 'Zeke' that he had spotted over Okayama, some 7000 ft below them. Seizing the moment, Baker simply drew up to within 75 yards of the unsuspecting fighter and fired an accurate burst that caused it to explode within seconds. This was his fourth, and last, victory in the P-47D.

The following afternoon the 41st FS performed yet another sweep of Formosa, and three kills were claimed by the unit's pilots. Two of these (a 'Hamp' and an 'Oscar') were credited to Lt James Mugavero, taking his final wartime tally to six. With P-47 operations thereafter rapidly tailing off, this pair of victories made the 24-year-old Mugavero the last pilot within the Fifth Air Force to be crowned an ace in the Thunderbolt.

Maj Dunham seems suitably happy with his contribution to the success of the 348th FG at the end of his tour in early 1945

P-51s IN THE PHILIPPINES

With the demise of the Fifth Air Force's P-47s (in the fighter role at least) in March/April 1945, operations switched to the more advanced P-51D Mustang for the final months of the war. Large-scale deployment of the new fighter did not commence until April, when the 348th and 35th FGs finally completed their respective work-ups in preparation for frontline service. Despite there being relatively few opportunities for pilots to exploit their new fighters' proven prowess against their Japanese counterparts, the handful of engagements that did take place nevertheless reinforced the already impeccable reputation the P-51D had earned for itself in the European war.

The versatility of the Mustang in comparison with the Thunderbolt was quickly brought to bear in the weeks after the first examples appeared over the Philippines. Preceding the re-equipment of the much larger fighter groups, the specialist 71st Tactical Reconnaissance Group (TRG), – and more specifically the 82nd Tactical Reconnaissance Squadron (TRS) – had replaced its venerable photo-optimised P-39N-2s with a handful of camera-equipped Mustang F-6Ds just prior to moving to Leyte from Biak, off New Guinea, in early November 1944.

Now flying a state-of-the-art aircraft capable of fighting its way into a target area to take all important pre- and post-raid photographs, the F-6D

Above and left
These views show the F-6D used by Capt William Shomo to shoot down six Ki-61 'Tony' fighters and a lone G4M 'Betty' bomber on 11 January 1945. By the time the lower photo was taken, the Mustang had had its fin cap painted yellow to denote its attachment to the 82nd TRS
(*Krane files*)

Capt Shomo's well-tanned crew chief Ralph Winkle poses by the nose of *SNOOKS-5th* soon after the aircraft's famous sortie (*Krane*)

pilots revelled in the performance of their new mounts during a series of missions (flown either as singletons or in two-ship formations) that probed ever deeper into Japanese-held territory. It was not long before the enemy was encountered, and the first significant Fifth Air Force Mustang kills achieved.

Although in combat in the Southwest Pacific from late 1943 until war's end, the 82nd TRS scored just 18 kills whilst undertaking its aerial reconnaissance mission. However, the unit's top ace was credited with no fewer than eight of these victories, which he scored during the course of

Right and below
Although William Shomo used F-6D-10 44-14841 to score all of his kills, most of the surviving photos of the Medal of Honor winner and his Mustang feature P-51D-20 44-72505, which was nicknamed *The FLYING UNDERTAKER*. This aircraft was allocated to Shomo soon after his epic sortie, and was given a first-class paint job in anticipation of press coverage of its pilot's feat

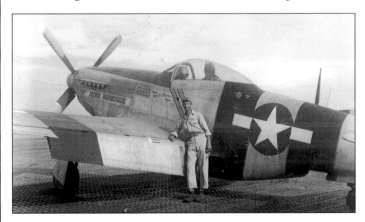

This publicity photo shows Capt Shomo overseeing the painting of eight victory flags forward of the cockpit of *SNOOKS-5th*

just two sorties separated by 24 hours. This incredible feat also won him the Congressional Medal of Honor.

Pennsylvanian Capt William Shomo had joined the 82nd TRS/71st TRG in November 1943, just weeks after the group had arrived in New Guinea. Flying many missions in both P-39Ns and P-40Ns, he was promoted to captain in September 1944, and became the CO of the 82nd TRS on Christmas Eve. Shomo had been in command of the 82nd TRS for a little over two weeks when he led an armed reconnaissance sweep over Tuguegarao airstrip, on Luzon, on the morning of 10 January that found a lone 'Val' dive-bomber circling over the field. He swiftly manoeuvred his F-6D-10 in behind the lumbering Aichi and shot it down, thus scoring the Mustang's first victory in the area.

The following day found Capt Shomo again in the same area (in F-6D-10 44-14841), leading Lt Paul Lipscomb (flying F-6D-15 44-14873) on an armed photo-recce of Atarri and Laoag airstrips in the hope of finding more enemy aircraft 'on the wing'. His hopes would be realised more handsomely than he could have ever imagined . . .

Cruising along the northern coast of Luzon, the two Mustang pilots came across a lone 'Betty' bomber, heavily defended by 11 Ki-61s and a lone Ki-44 in formation some 2000 ft above it. Using the F-6D's superb rate of climb, Shomo immediately took the initiative by rushing headlong into the midst of the unsuspecting escorts. Just prior to despatching two of the 'Tonys', both pilots had witnessed some of their opponents actually 'waggling' their wings in greeting as the Mustangs closed on them! The Japanese pilots must have thought that the inline-engined F-6Ds were more Ki-61 escorts arriving in support of the 'Betty', since the shape of the

Lt Paul 'Lippy' Lipscomb was Capt Shomo's wingman during the 11 January sortie. Flying F-6D-15 44-14873, he originally claimed as many as five Japanese aircraft shot down, but this tally was later revised to three – these were Lipscomb's only kills of the war

Capt William Shomo poses in the cockpit of *SNOOKS-5th* just days after his seven-kill mission . . .

Mustang had not yet been encountered by the army air force in the Southwest Pacific.

Pulling back into the formation after completing his first devastating pass, Shomo had 'bagged' a third Ki-61 before the surviving Japanese pilots finally reacted more in confusion than with any co-ordinated attempt to counter the two F-6Ds decimating their ranks. In the general bedlam which then ensued, the 'Betty' tried to escape by diving towards a nearby Japanese airfield, but just as it was closing on the runway, Shomo got in a good burst from below the bomber which caused it to explode and crash.

Despite having already claimed four kills (and thus become an ace), Shomo was just warming to the idea of being a 'proper' fighter pilot. Searching out further targets, he was suddenly set upon by a lone Ki-44 'Tojo' that he had failed to spot, and it took all his flying skills to evade a series of well-aimed deflection shots before the Japanese pilot decided upon a wiser course of action and dived away to safety. Galvanised by his close shave, Shomo chased down a further three Ki-61s and added these to his previous successes. His wingman, Lt Paul Lipscomb, was also kept busy throughout the engagement destroying three 'Tonys'.

With all the Ki-61s having either been shot down or scared off, the two tactical-recce pilots completed the rout of the enemy by circling the area and taking pictures of the smouldering wrecks in the jungle below.

Promoted to major just three days after this action, William Shomo was awarded the Medal of Honor for his part in the one-sided mission. Spectacular one-off engagements like this would be the only way that P-51D pilots could achieve ace status in the Philippines in the final months of the war, for the enemy was now rarely encountered in the skies.

Reflecting the Fifth Air Force's mood in 1945, Gen Kenney joked soon after the 11 January engagement that Japanese morale would have

. . . and is then seen strapping into *The FLYING UNDERTAKER* at Binmaley some weeks later. The lighter stripe bordering the black unit markings just behind the cockpit has often been interpreted as being yellow in colour, but it is now widely believed to be black paint oversprayed onto tape residue left over from the fuselage masking

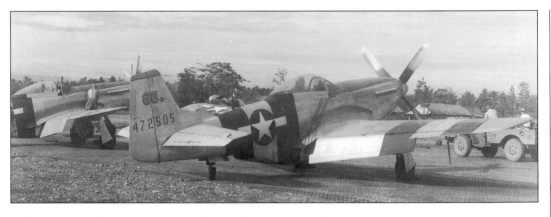

suffered even further had they known that Paul Lipscomb had been a cowboy in civilian life, and William Shomo a licensed embalmer!

P-51s FOR P-47 ACES

As the war in the Pacific drew to its inevitable climax, the sighting of Japanese aircraft in the air became the exception rather than the rule. Facing overwhelming air superiority, few army or navy fighters attempted to challenge the P-51D upon its arrival in numbers on Luzon. Occasionally, there was the chance encounter with an individual reconnaissance aircraft, but the days of the big air battles were no well and truly over.

Aside from being issued to the long-established fighter groups like the 348th and 5th FGs, P-51s were also utilised by the newly-formed 3rd Air Commando Group (ACG), and its 3rd and 4th Air Commando Squadrons (ACS). Trained to be highly mobile, tasked with supporting troops on the ground and also equipped with C-47 transports and L-5 observation aircraft, the 3rd ACG was the last of three such groups created between March and May 1944 for eventual combat in the CBI and the Pacific.

The 3rd ACG was the only one to see action in the latter theatre, with its two fighter units (redesignated Fighter Squadrons (Combat) prior to arriving in the Philippines) being initially based at Leyte in December 1944, before moving closer to the action at Mangaldan (on Luzon) in late January 1945.

Starboard view of the much-photographed *The FLYING UNDERTAKER* at Binmaley in the early spring of 1945

This more standard P-51D of the 82nd PRS lacks nose art and the two yellow stripes below the cockpit which made Capt Shomo's Mustang so distinctive. It is possible that an enthusiastic Gen Kenney allowed the latter's P-51D to be painted in its one-off scheme specially for the press cameras

Capt Louis Curdes smiles proudly for the camera in 'his' P-51D-20 (44-62272) in February 1945. His scoreboard shows unique mix of Axis and Allied victories, the 'Old Glory' denoting his claim against a USAAF C-47. He had been forced to shoot the latter aircraft down when its pilot mistakenly attempted to land on a Japanese-held island. Curdes fretted about the consequences for him, and the fate of the people aboard the transport, but the C-47's occupants were all rescued safely (including a female acquaintance of the P-51 pilot) and returned to American control. The ace was subsequently commended for his presence of mind (*USAF*)

The tally of aerial kills achieved by the 3rd ACG accurately reflects the lack of targets encountered by Mustang pilots in the final months of the conflict, the combined score for both squadrons and the group's staff flight totalling just 16 destroyed and four damaged by VJ-Day. Scoring one of the first of these kills was 3rd FS(C) boss, and ex-Eighth Air Force ace, Maj Walker 'Bud' Mahurin (see *Osprey Aircraft of the Aces 24 - P-47 Thunderbolt Aces of the Eighth Air Force* for details). One of the leading P-47 aces in the European Theatre of Operations, Mahurin had scored 19.75 kills by the time he was shot down over France on 27 March 1944 and forced to evade, with the help of the French Resistance – he was delivered back to the Allies on 7 May.

Upon his return to England, Mahurin was prevented from returning to operations with his unit (the 56th FG) by an Eighth Air Force ruling created to help protect the identities of his French rescuers. It was feared that if captured, Mahurin (or any other evading pilot) could crack under interrogation, thus placing the lives of those that had hidden him in great danger.

Sent back to the USA, Mahurin refused to see out the war as an instructor, and instead actively sought out a posting that would swiftly see him back into action . . . but this time against the Japanese. He soon found just the job with the recently-created 3rd ACG, being given command of the group's 3rd FS(C) during its final stages of pre-deployment work-ups. Leading his Mustang-equipped squadron across the Pacific in late November, Mahurin commenced operation over the Philippines just prior to Christmas.

Although dismayed at the paucity of aerial targets, it didn't take the

Maj Walker M Mahurin added a solitary Japanese kill to his impressive tally of victories in the ETO flying this P-51D-15 (44-14978) whilst in command of the 3rd ACS in the Philippines. His 'Dinah' kill of 14 January 1945 made him one of a relatively select group of American pilots to score in excess of 20 victories (*Michael O'Leary*)

This line-up shot of distinctively-marked P-51Ds of the 35th FG was almost certainly taken at Clark Field judging by the mountainous backdrop. Note that the nose and tail markings differ between the Mustangs in the photo, denoting that aircraft from more than one squadron are featured in this shot

veteran ace long to score his first (and only) kill with the P-51D. Maj Mahurin was leading a sweep over northern Luzon on the morning of 14 January 1945 when he and another pilot in his flight sighted several Ki-46 'Dinahs' flying near Bagabag airstrip. Despite having failed to see an enemy aircraft in his sights since late March 1944, Mahurin's 'killer instincts' quickly came to the fore and he latched onto the tail of the Japanese reconnaissance aircraft and shot it down. A second Ki-46 was also credited to Lt Charles Adams, who chased his quarry for 15 miles before finally destroying it.

Like the 348th FG's Lt George Davis, 'Bud' Mahurin would go on to enjoy more success over Korea (3.5 MiG-15s, one probable and one damaged) flying F-86Es with both the 51st and 4th FIGs, before being shot down by flak and captured in May 1952.

UNUSUAL MUSTANG VICTORY

'Bud' Mahurin was not the only ace to score a victory whilst flying with the 3rd ACG, for fellow European PoW/escapee Lt Louis Curdes also

P-51D 44-72198 of Maj M R Beamer breaks away from the camera in mid-1945. Beamer was CO of the 41st FS during the final months of the Pacific war

downed a 'Dinah' during his tour with the 4th FS(C) on 7 February 1945. Already an eight-victory ace with the Mediterranean-based, P-38-equipped, 82nd FG (see *Osprey Aircraft of the Aces 19 - P-38 Lightning Aces of the ETO/MTO* for details) by the time he was forced to bail out over Italy with mechanical trouble, Curdes spent less than a fortnight in a PoW camp before escaping and living behind German lines until crossing into Allied territory in May 1944. Repatriated to the USA, he successfully applied for a transfer to the 3rd ACG and accompanied the group to the Philippines in late 1944.

Although Lt Curdes' 'Dinah' kill was his final Axis victory, it did not signal the end of his scoring run. On 10 February, whilst on a sweep to Batan Island (mid way between Luzon and Formosa), a member of his flight was forced to parachute into the sea and Curdes circled above to

The pilot of P-51D-20 44-64055 trudges away from the wreckage of his fighter carrying his parachute and lifejacket after coming to grief either taking off or landing sometime during 1945. The 'star and bar' on this 3rd ACG aircraft seems to have been painted onto a field of white between the black bands on the fuselage

Lacking identifying unit symbols on their rudders, it is difficult to tell whether these P-51Ds hail from the 71st TRG or the 3rd ACS

guide the resulting rescue efforts. While flying over the downed airman, Curdes spotted a USAAF C-47 that appeared to be intent on landing at the Japanese-held airfield on Batan. Although the ace attempted to shepherd the transport away from the airstrip, he met with little success. He then decided on the only action left open to him – the shoot it down.

Using all his skill, Curdes clinically shot out each engine, leaving the C-47 pilot with little option but to ditch the stricken transport in the calm seas. The 13 people aboard the transport, as well as the downed P-51 pilot, were all subsequently rescued and returned to Luzon.

Irma VIII was the personal mount of Capt Anthony Faikus of the 40th FS

For some days after this highly unusual action, Curdes was anxious about the consequences of his unorthodox approach to stopping the C-47. He need not have concerned himself, however, for he was not only cleared but commended by his superiors for his quick thinking in a crisis situation. For a time, Lt Curdes' P-51D-20 44-63272 *Bad Angel* boasted seven swastikas, an Italian fasces, a Japanese 'rising sun' and an American flag! He was later reassigned to the 49th FG, and the very familiar P-38, but he did not add to his score.

IE SHIMA

With little prospect of action over the Philippines by mid-1945, the P-51-equipped 348th and 35th FGs moved to their final wartime base on the tiny island of Ie Shima, off the recently-won island of Okinawa, in July 1945. The commanders of the newly-reformed Far East Air Forces (FEAF) were keen to commit the combat units of both the Fifth and Thirteenth Air Forces to action over the Japanese home islands, and the Mustang pilots were eager to oblige.

However, targets again proved elusive, although the 40th FS's Lt Ellis Baker did succeed in downing two Kawanishi N1K2-J 'George' fighters for his fifth and sixth victories during a sweep over the Japanese coast near Kyushu on 5 July. The 40th FS actually destroyed four of these brand new navy fighters during this engagement, the pair credited to Baker being his final kills of the war.

Although of poor quality, this photograph neverthless shows the P-51D of P-47 ace Capt George Della. A veteran of almost two years in combat when this shot was taken in the spring of 1945, Della had 'made ace' on Christmas Eve 1944 flying with the 460th FS

A further three 348th FG aces scored their last victories when the group turned its attentions to the Indo-China coast, Formosa and Japan itself in search of new targets. One of these individuals was none other than veteran P-47 ace, and now group Deputy Commander, Lt

348th FG CO Col Dick Rowland is seen in the cockpit of his P-51D-15 (44-15103). He commanded the group from November 1943 until June 1945 (*Vickers*)

Col 'Dinghy' Dunham, who had rejoined his beloved 348th FG after completing a gunnery course in the USA in January 1945 – he had initially been posted back to the group in May as its Operation Officer, having briefly held the post of Assistant Operations Officer from December 1944 until his return to America the following month.

A man of action to the end, Dunham was far from content with administrative duties back at Ie Shima while the shooting war continued, and on 1 August 1945, flying a brand new P-51K-10, he led 342nd FS CO (and five-kill ace), Maj Ed Popek, and two wingmen on a sweep of the home island of Kyushu.

Approaching the southern coast of the target area at a height in excess of 16,000 ft, Dunham spotted a formation of B-24s 5000 ft below them, coming under attack by 20 Japanese fighters as they passed over Take Island. He immediately led his Mustangs into the fray with no particular plan except to save the American bombers. The enemy fighters were swiftly identified as Ki-84 'Franks' – the ultimate army fighter of the war, and a type rarely encountered by the 348th FG in the Philippines.

Despite the fighter's formidable reputation, 'Dinghy' Dunham had both superior speed and two years of combat experience on his side. With one good burst of machine gun fire, he shattered the glass canopy of the first 'Frank' that appeared in his gunsight and almost certainly killed its pilot, for the Japanese fighter dived straight into the sea. This victory took Lt Col Dunham's final tally to 16, with no probables or damaged claims.

Ed Popek also enjoyed success during this engagement, tackling several Ki-84s that had climbed away from the B-24s and then scattered upon sighting the quartet of diving Mustangs. The major quickly latched on to

'Dinghy' Dunham's immaculately presented P-51D *"MRS. BONNIE"* is seen in August 1945 following the application of the veteran pilot's final kill marking (*Schubert*)

Above and top
P-51K-10 44-12073 *SUNSHINE VII*
was flown by 348th FG CO Col
William Banks during the final
weeks of the war. Colourful stripes
on the aircraft's spinner and through
its nickname represented each of
the four squadrons within the group
(the 348th FG was the only group
within V FC to control four units). In
the lower shot, Col Banks (left)
stands alongside his crew chief,
'Doc' Alston
(*Norman Taylor via Krane files*)

Seen just weeks after VJ-Day, this
F-6K was flown by 110th TRS boss
Maj George Noland, who took
charge of the unit in May 1945. He
almost certainly claimed the last
victories credited to a
reconnaissance unit during World
War 2 when he downed three
Japanese aircraft on 14 August
1945. Later assessments apparently
reduced one claim to a probable

a 'Frank' performing a tight turn, and he duly waited for it to straighten out, before firing at close range and sending the fighter earthwards trailing smoke and with an undercarriage leg hanging free.

The battle then degenerated into a series of individual dogfights, with the P-51 pilots firing at anything that appeared in their gunsights, whilst their Japanese counterparts desperately attempted to use their superior numbers to get onto the tails of the outnumbered American fighters, who were employing solid two-aircraft section tactics. The latter paid off handsomely when Maj Popek's wingman, Lt Thomas Sheets, 'bagged' a wildly manoeuvring 'Frank' that his leader failed to destroy. The major later recorded in his combat report;

'I spotted another ("Frank") and chased him, but he started a steep turn before I could get in a burst. The other P-51, which was flown by Lt Sheets, got in a burst but did not get him. I then took another pass but missed. Lt Sheets missed his next pass, but set the "Frank" up for me. I came down at a 45° angle and about a 55° deflection shot, and put a solid burst into his cockpit. His cockpit seemed to crumble up and he crashed into the sea. We both fought with him from 10,000 ft down to 2000 ft.

'The "Frank" is a very manoeuvrable ship, but we could out-run it and outdive it. No one tried to outclimb it.'

Maj Ed Popek was credited with two kills upon his return to Ie Shima, thus taking his final tally to seven destroyed.

P-51s OF THE FOURTEENTH AIR FORCE

Confirming that the CBI really was the 'forgotten front' of World War 2 (at least in the minds of senior Allied strategists), the P-51A saw its first action in China just days prior to the much improved P-51B being cleared for operations in the ETO with the Pioneer Mustang Group (354th FG) as part of the Eighth Air Force's VIII FC.

Performing a Thanksgiving Day raid on Shinchiku airfield, on the island of Formosa, on 25 November 1943, the Allison-engined A-models belonged to the 23rd FG, which could trace its roots back to the legendary 1st American Volunteer Group (AVG) of 1941. With the replacement of its venerable P-40 Warhawks with early-model Mustangs, one of the few vestiges of the 'Flying Tiger' spirit still present within the 23rd FG was its new CO, Lt Col David Lee 'Tex' Hill. He had flown with the 1st AVG's 2nd Pursuit Squadron and then its USAAF replacement (the 75th FS/23rd FG)

Wearing the 311th FG's distinctive badge beneath its cockpit, this P-51B-10 was assigned to the 529th FS at Pungchacheng, in China, in early 1945. Note the P-40Ns parked in the distance (*Michael O'Leary*)

Wearing the nickname *PRINCESS* beneath its exhaust stubs, this P-51C-10 (42-103896) was photographed from a C-47 during an escort mission over China on 24 July 1945. Its twin (yellow) tail stripes denote that it was assigned to the 311th FG's 530th FS (*Michael O'Leary*)

Gen Claire Chennault (standing with his hands behind his back, wearing a leather A-2 jacket) addresses pilots of the 23rd FG soon after the arrival of the first P-51B in-theatre. Note how the aircraft has already been adorned with the trademark 'sharksmouth' of the former AVG (*Michael O'Leary*)

Maj David L 'Tex' Hill, A-2 jacket firmly buttoned up, prepares for a mission in his 75th FS/23rd FG P-51B in the autumn of 1944. Following the completion of his second tour in China, Hill returned to the USA in October 1944 and took command of the Bell YP-59-equipped 412th FG – the USAAF's first jet unit. Upon leaving the service in 1945, he joined the Texas Air National Guard

until sent back to America suffering from dysentery and malaria in November 1942.

Hill scored 13.25 kills in P-40C/Es during his 11 months in Burma and China, and upon his recovery, expressed a strong desire to go back into combat in the CBI. Returning to the theatre as the 23rd FG's new CO just as the first P-51A-1s were arriving at the group's Kweilin base in

early November 1943, Hill immediately took it upon himself to personally oversee the conversion of the group's three squadron's (starting with the 76th FS) from the obsolescent Warhawk to the more capable Mustang.

Following a hasty work-up, 'Tex' Hill looked for a suitably impressive target against which the Mustang could make its combat debut, and after studying recent aerial photos of the airfield at Shinchiku, on Formosa, he decided that this was it.

The various images shot by an F-5 Lightning on 24 November showed the airfield jam packed with over 200 fighters and bombers.

The Japanese may have felt secure on Formosa, for the short range of the P-40 had meant that bombers attempting to strike at Shinchiku had to do so unescorted. However, this had all changed with the recent arrival of a handful of P-38Gs and P-51As, and Lt Col Hill decided that a surprise strike on the airfield by a mixed force of 14 B-25s, eight P-51s of the 76th FS and eight P-38s from the 449th FS would effectively announce the arrival of both the Mustang and Lightning in-theatre.

His plan called for the P-38s to directly escort the B-25s and the P-51s to strafe one side of the airfield while the B-25s bombed the other. In order to maximise the element of surprise, *(text continues on page 65)*

Zero-length rocket tube-equipped P-51C *IOWA Belle* was flown by Lt Curtiss Mahanna of the 75th FS/23rd FG. This pilot scored three confirmed and three probable kills in the final months of the war with the Mustang, and would have surely 'made ace' had their been more Japanese aircraft still flying in 1945 (*W Hess*)

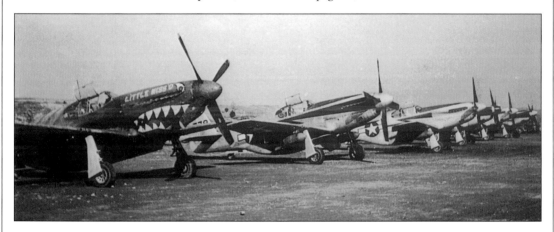

A lone 74th FS Mustang heads a row of bombed up 118th TRS P-51Cs. Note the faded 1st ACG fuselage bands on the former fighter

This close-up of a well-weathered Mustang from the 118th TRS shows off the squadron's distinctive lightning bolt marking. Inevitably nicknamed the 'Black Lightning Squadron', the 118th picked out their 'bolt with yellow paint (*W Hess*)

COLOUR PLATES

This colour section profiles the P-47 Thunderbolts and P-51 Mustangs flown by the aces of the Pacific and CBI, as well as six representative figures showing the uniforms worn by these elite pilots. All the artwork has been specially commissioned for this volume, and profile artist Tom Tullis and figure artist Mike Chappell have gone to great pains to illustrate the aircraft, and their pilots, as accurately as possible

following exhaustive original research by the author. Few of the aircraft depicted on the following pages have been illustrated in colour artwork before, and the schemes shown here have been fully authenticated either by the pilot(s) who flew the aircraft in combat, or from contemporary official images taken by USAAF photographers or aviators/groundcrews serving in-theatre during World War 2

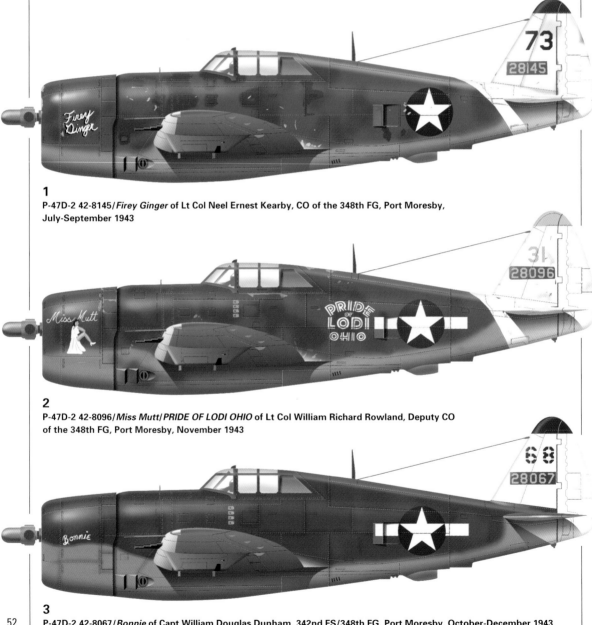

1
P-47D-2 42-8145/*Firey Ginger* of Lt Col Neel Ernest Kearby, CO of the 348th FG, Port Moresby, July-September 1943

2
P-47D-2 42-8096/*Miss Mutt*/*PRIDE OF LODI OHIO* of Lt Col William Richard Rowland, Deputy CO of the 348th FG, Port Moresby, November 1943

3
P-47D-2 42-8067/*Bonnie* of Capt William Douglas Dunham, 342nd FS/348th FG, Port Moresby, October-December 1943

4
P-47D-4 42-22684/*Miss Mutt II*/*PRIDE OF LODI OHIO* of Lt Col William Richard Rowland, CO of the 348th FG, Finschhafen, December 1943

5
P-47D-11 42-22903/*"Kathy"*/*VENI VIDI VICI* of Lt Lawrence O'Neill, 342nd FS/348th FG, Finschhafen, December 1943

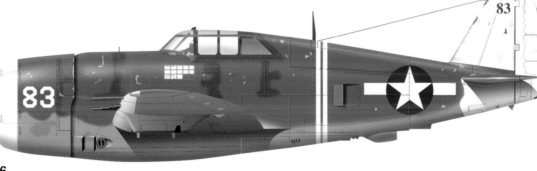

6
P-47D-4 (serial unknown) of Maj Gerald R Johnson, CO of the 9th FS/49th FG, Nadzab, January 1944

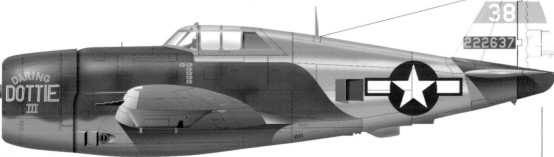

7
P-47D-3 42-22637/*DARING DOTTIE III* of Maj John T Moore, CO of the 341st FS/348th FG, Finschhafen, February-March 1944

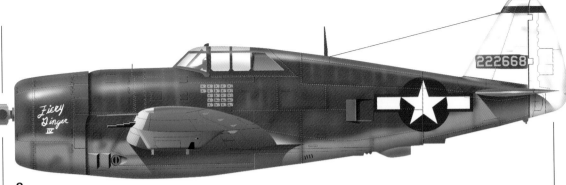

8
P-47D-4 42-22668/*Fiery Ginger IV* of Col Neel E Kearby, V Fighter Command, Finschhafen, March 1944

9
P-47D-11 42-22855/*HOYT'S HOSS* of Lt Edward R Hoyt, 41st FS/35th FG, Gusap, March 1944

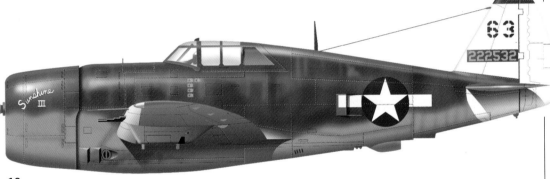

10
P-47D-2 42-22532/*Sunshine III* of Capt William M Banks, CO of the 342nd FS/348th FG, Finschhafen, February-June 1944

11
P-51A-10 43-6189 of Col Phillip Cochran, CO of the 1st Air Commando Group, Hailakandi, March-May 1944

12
P-47D-23 43-27899/*JOSIE* of Lt Mike Dikovitsky, 340th FS/348th FG, Leyte, December 1944

13
P-51A-1 43-6077/*Jackie* of Capt James John England, 530th FS/311th FG, Dinjan, May 1944

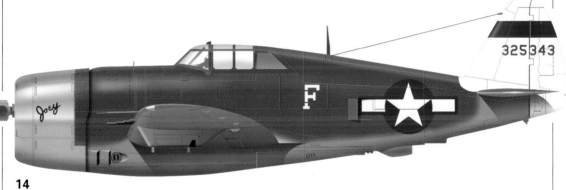

14
P-47D-21 43-25343/*Joey* of Lt William Mathis, 19th FS/318th FG, Saipan, June 1944

15
P-47D-23 43-27861 of Lt LeRoy V Grossheusch, 39th FS/35th FG, Morotai, September 1944

16
P-51C (serial and sub-type unknown) *Little Jeep* of Capt Forrest H Parham, 75th FS/23rd FG, Luliang,
November 1944

17
P-51C (serial and sub-type unknown) *LOPE'S HOPE 3rd* of Lt Donald S Lopez, 75th FS/23rd FG, Kweilin,
September 1944

18
P-51B-7 (probably 43-7060) *Tommy's Dad* of Maj John C Herbst, CO of the 74th FS/23rd FG, Luliang,
January 1945

19
P-51C (serial and sub-type unknown) *IOWA BELLE* of Lt Curtiss W Mahanna, 75th FS/23rd FG, Luliang, January 1945

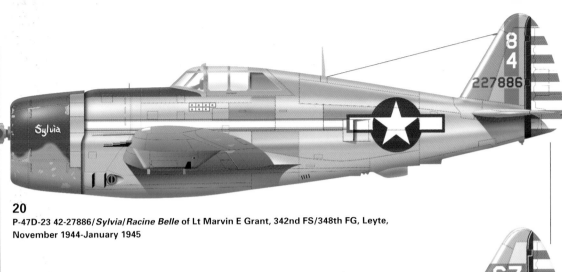

20
P-47D-23 42-27886/*Sylvia*/*Racine Belle* of Lt Marvin E Grant, 342nd FS/348th FG, Leyte,
November 1944-January 1945

21
P-47D-25 42-28110/*My Baby* of Capt Alvaro Jay Hunter, 40th FS/35th FG, Pitoe, December 1944-January 1945

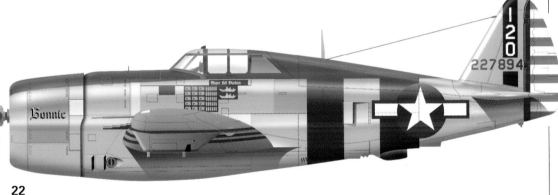

22
P-47D-25, 42-27894/*Bonnie* of Maj William D Dunham, CO of the 460th FS/348th FG, Leyte, December 1944

23
P-47D-28 42-28505/*My Baby* of Capt Alvaro Jay Hunter, 40th FS/35th FG, October-December 1944

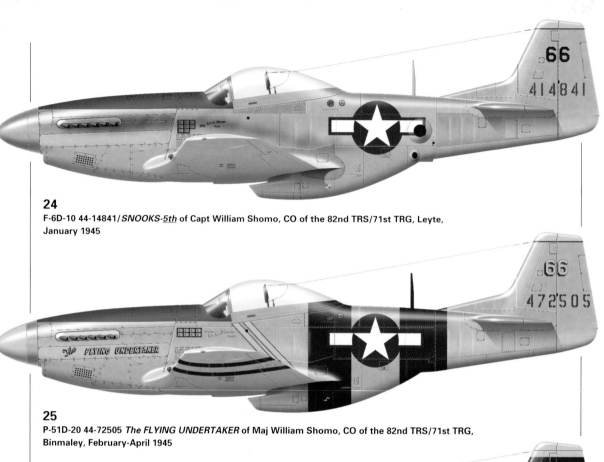

24
F-6D-10 44-14841/*SNOOKS-5th* of Capt William Shomo, CO of the 82nd TRS/71st TRG, Leyte,
January 1945

25
P-51D-20 44-72505 *The FLYING UNDERTAKER* of Maj William Shomo, CO of the 82nd TRS/71st TRG,
Binmaley, February-April 1945

26
P-51D-20 44-63984/*Margaret IV* of Maj James Buckley Tapp, CO of the 78th FS/15th FG, Iwo Jima
(South Field), April-May 1945

27
P-51D-20 44-63483/*Stinger VII* of Maj Robert W Moore, 45th FS/15th FG, Iwo Jima (South Field), June 1945

28
P-51D (serial and sub-type unknown) of Maj Clyde B Slocumb, CO of the 75th FS/23rd FG, Luliang,
April-August 1945

29
P-51B-15 42-106908 of Lt Leonard R Reeves, 530th FS/311th FG, Pungchacheng, January 1945

30
P-51C-10 42-103285/*JANIE* of Lt Lester Muenster, 530th FS/311th FG, Pungchacheng, January 1945

31
P-51D-10 44-14626 of Lt Col Edward O McComas, CO of the 118th TRS/23rd FG, Luliang, January 1945

32
P-51D-10 44-11276 of Lt Col Charles H Older, 23rd FG, Luliang, June 1945

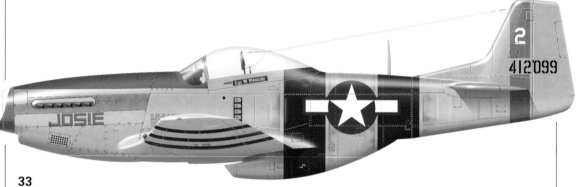

33
P-51K-10 44-12099/*JOSIE* of Lt Michael Dikovitsky, 340th FS/348th FG, San Marcelino, January 1945

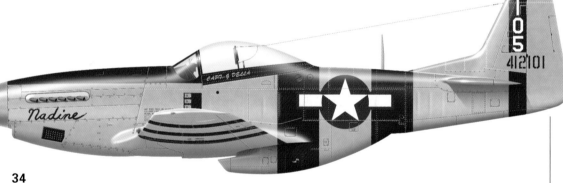

34
P-51K-10 44-12101/*Nadine* of Capt George Della, 460th FS/348th FG, Floridablance, May-June 1945

35
P-51K-10 44-12073/*SUNSHINE VII* of Lt Col William T Banks, CO of the 348th FG, Ie Shima, July 1945

36
P-51D-20 44-75623/*My Ach'in!* of Maj Harry C Crim, CO of the 531st FS/21st FG, Iwo Jima, July 1945

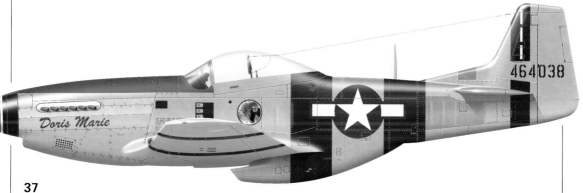

37
P-51D-20 44-64038/*Doris Marie* of Lt Thomas Sheets, 460th FS/348th FG, Ie Shima, August 1945

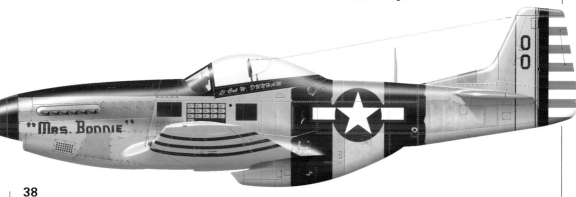

38
P-51K-10 44-12017/*"Mrs. Bonnie"* of Lt Col William D Dunham, 348th FG, Ie Shima, August 1945

39
P-47N-1 44-88211/*Lil Meaties' MEAT CHOPPER* of Lt Oscar Perdomo, 464th FS/507th FG, Ie Shima, August 1945

P-51K-10 44-12833/ *"WE THREE"* of Maj George Noland, CO of the 110th TRS/71st TRG, Ie Shima, August 1945

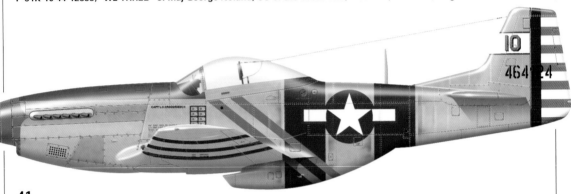

41
P-51D-20 44-64124 of Capt LeRoy Grossheusch, CO of the 39th FS/35th FG, Okinawa, August 1945

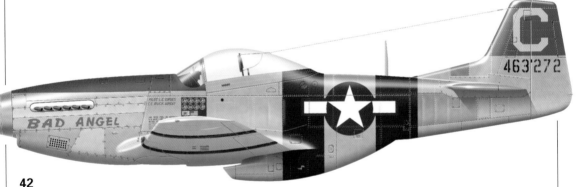

42
P-51D-20 44-63272/ *BAD ANGEL* of Lt Louis E Curdes, 4th FS(C)/3rd ACG, Laoag, August 1945

1
Lt Robert H Knapp, 342nd FS/348th FG, Saidor, May 1944

2
Lt Lawrence O'Neill, 342nd FS/348th FG, Finschhafen, December 1943

3
Lt Oscar Perdomo, 464th FS/507th FG, Ie Shima, August 1945

4
Lt Col Edward O McComas, CO of
the 118th TRS/23rd FG, Luliang,
January 1945

5
Maj John C Herbst, CO of the 74th
FS/23rd FG, Luliang, January 1945

6
Lt Lester L Arasmith, 530th
FS/311th FG, Pungchacheng,
March 1945

the approach to the target would be made at minimum altitude across the straits between Suichan, on the coast of China, and Shinchiku.

Closing on the target at a height of about 30 ft, the USAAF force arrived over the airfield completely unannounced, and proceeded to inflict serious damage on the myriad aircraft lined up all over the base.

None of the attackers were lost during the raid, and 14 Japanese aircraft that were either in the pattern over the airfield, or had scrambled in an attempt to repel the Americans, were scythed down by the P-38s and P-51s. A further 30+ aircraft on the ground were also claimed destroyed.

Although the bulk of the kills both in the air (12) and on the ground (12) went to the Lightning pilots of the 449th FS, the 76th also made a significant contribution to the tally. Appropriately, the first kill credited to the P-51A in China fell to 'Tex' Hill himself after he went to the aid of a B-25 that he had spotted was under attack from a Ki-43. The 'Oscar' was climbing steeply after hurriedly taking off and had just started to turn in behind the bomber when Hill hit it with a burst of fire so accurate that the fighter exploded. He then reverted to the strafing role, destroying one parked aircraft and probably destroying a second.

With the airfield littered with smoking wrecks, and the sky overhead swept clear of Japanese aircraft, Lt Col Hill issued the command to withdraw back across the straits to China. Just as he in turn pointed his Mustang north-westwards, he felt what he initially though was a bullet hit his fighter. Hill immediately took evasive action to lose the unseen enemy on his tail, and almost flew into the sea in the process. The 'enemy' seemingly vanished as soon as it had appeared, and the remainder of the flight back to Kweilin passed without event. Upon landing, one of Hill's armourers quickly pointed out that the bullet that had 'struck' his P-51 was in fact one of his own rounds detonating in the ammunition tray due to the intense levels of heat generated by the rapidity of his firing over the target!

'Tex' Hill later described this mission as having been 'perfectly executed', and from then on he developed an affection for the P-51 in combat that was rivalled only by his attachment to the P-40.

The first few months of 1944 saw the successful Thanksgiving Day debut slowly built upon as a steady trickle of P-51As (and a handful of B-models) arrived at Kweilin, and by June there were more Mustangs in-theatre with the Fourteenth Air Force than P-40s. However, due to the CBI's low priority for the receipt of new equipment, the conversion of the 23rd FG onto the P-51 took an agonisingly long time to complete, which in turn hampered the generation of Mustang aces in China.

Despite its paucity in numbers, the A-model Mustang nevertheless left an indelible impression on the enemy, particularly when flown by a pilot of the calibre of veteran 23rd FG P-40 ace, Capt John Stewart.

Although of indifferent quality, this rare view shows five-kill ace Capt 'Pappy' Parham of the 75th FS taxiing out in his P-51C *Little Jeep* at Luliang in late 1944. Having downed four aircraft in the P-40N in the late summer of 1944, Parham 'made ace' (almost certainly in this aircraft) on 11 November when he destroyed a 'Hamp'

Again of poor quality, this shot nevertheless features an ace's aircraft in the shape of Lt Leonard 'Randy' Reeves' P-51C *My Dallas Darlin*. Seen on an escort mission to Peiping (Bei Jing) in late January 1945, this 530th FS Mustang was used by Reeves to score his last kills on 25 March 1945 (*Carl Fischer*)

Lt Lester Arasmith had been with the 530th FS just a matter of weeks when the unit moved with the 311th FG to China from Burma in August 1944. Whilst flying with the Fourteenth Air Force, he would score six kills in this P-51C between 17 November 1944 and 24 March 1945 (*Wolf*)

Lt 'Randy' Reeves was another 530th FS ace who scored all six of his kills flying P-51Cs over China in 1944-45 (*Wolf*)

A member of the 76th FS since August 1942, he had scored seven kills in P-40K/Ms by the time he was made CO on 1 December 1943 (in place of fellow ace Capt J M Williams, who was shot down in his P-51A on this date by a Japanese fighter during a mission to Hong Kong – he successfully evaded and was duly returned to the USA).

By the time Stewart assumed command of the 76th FS, it had already become the first unit in the 23rd FG to swap its Warhawks for Mustangs, and he quickly became an avid proponent of the latter aircraft – to the point where he went on record and stated that 'the air war in China began with the introduction of this new type'.

Capt Stewart's initial success with the fighter took the form of a Zero claimed as a probable on 27 December 1943 over Suichwan airfield, and his first confirmed kill followed 15 days later when he destroyed a Ki-48 'Lily' bomber in the same area. On 10 February 1944 he damaged a Zero in the vicinity of Kiukiang, and 48 hours later shot an 'Oscar' down (which he identified as a Ki-44 'Tojo' in his mission report) north of Kanchow when he came to the aid of 449th FS P-38s that were being attacked by about a dozen Japanese fighters;

'. . . the Jap saw us coming and started a sharp turn. He was visibly shaken when we outturned him, so he dove for the deck. We found that we could out-run him too, for when he levelled off at 100 ft above the deck, we steadily closed in on him. He tried evasive action, but it was to no avail. I got to close range, gave him about 70 rounds, and he exploded violently. One "Tojo" was eliminated, but best of all, we all knew we were flying a better fighter than the Japanese.'

Despite the frustration of having to struggle on with a modest force of P-51s, augmented by worn-out P-40s, 'Tex' Hill – supported by men of the calibre of John Stewart – continued to lead the 23rd FG by example through to mid-October 1944, when he returned to the USA tour-expired. Aside from his 'Oscar' kill on 25 November 1943, he scored one more confirmed victory in a P-51B on 6 May 1944 when he downed a 'Hamp' near Hankow (he damaged a second Mitsubishi fighter in the same engagement).

On 15 October 1944 Col 'Tex' Hill was replaced at the 'helm' of the 23rd FG (by Lt Col Philip Loofbourrow, who had previously commanded the 75th FS). Having scored 15.25 kills, one probable and six damaged, few individuals had done more to ensure an Allied victory in the air over China.

CHINA MUSTANG ACES

With sufficient Mustangs in place by mid-1944 to make a real impact in the air war over China, it comes as no surprise to find that the bulk of the kills credited to P-51 pilots in-theatre were scored during the second half of that year. The same attributes which made the fighter unbeatable in the ETO, MTO and the Pacific – range and outstanding performance – also resulted in a relative handful of Mustangs (five fighter groups, two of which were Chinese-American Composite Wings) in China quickly gaining aerial ascendancy over a depleted Japanese fighter force.

One of the first pilots to fully exploit the Packard Merlin-engined P-51B in combat over China was Lt Oran Watts of the 118th TRS, which had been assigned to the 23rd FG in mid-June 1944. Flying over Anking

Below
Leading China ace 'Pappy' Herbst and ground kill ace Maj Floyd Finberg (both from the 23rd FG) warm their hands over a stove at Luliang during the winter of 1944-45. Finberg claimed three aerial victories and 11 ground kills (*Wolf*)

Bottom
Maj Herbst poses in the cockpit of his P-51B-7 43-7060. Note the caps over the muzzles of the .50 cal guns in the wing and the white cross on the fuselage, the latter indicating the fitment of a fuselage fuel tank in this Mustang (*Michael O'Leary*)

on 7 July on an armed recce, Watts intercepted a formation of 'Oscars' on the outskirts of the city and proceeded to down two of them before the surviving fighters broke off the engagement. A third 'Oscar' fell to his guns over Lupao four days later, followed by a fourth Nakajima fighter (plus one damaged) during a sweep over Tanchuk on 14 July. Watts completed his scoring on 5 October when he downed a 'Tojo' whilst flying a P-51C over Sanshui, this final success making him the first of three pilots to attain ace status with the 118th TRS.

At around the time that Oran Watts was arriving at Kweilin with his unit, much-travelled fighter pilot Capt John C 'Pappy' Herbst was just about to commence an incredible scoring run that would see him down 18 aircraft in seven months with the 23rd FG. A lot older than most of his contemporaries in China, Herbst had been born in 1909 and acquired his nickname upon arriving in the frontline due to his relatively advanced age – although this also worked in his favour, for it won him a great deal of respect for his maturity, and experience as a pilot.

Capt Herbst had been working as a tax consultant for an oil company when he jumped at the opportunity to learn to fly with the Royal Canadian Air Force in 1941. Sent to Britain upon the completion of his training, he officially did not see any action in Europe, although the scoreboard on his P-51 would later feature a single swastika which certain sources claim denoted a Bf 109 kill in the Mediterranean.

Herbst returned to the USA in early 1942 and transferred into the USAAF, where he was given the job of flight instructing at a base on the Florida coast, much to his frustration. With his age and superb piloting skills conspiring to keep him firmly within Training Command, it was only through a chance meeting with a recuperating 'Tex' Hill that Herbst

Col Grant Mahony was a highly respected pilot who claimed one 'Oscar' in the air and several other Japanese aircraft on the ground flying Mustangs with the 23rd FG. Following the completion of his first combat tour, he subsequently went back into action in the Southwest Pacific with the 8th FG and was killed in January 1945 during a strafing run in his P-38 (*Hess*)

was sent to the frontline. The former happened to witness a superbly-flown, and highly illegal, aerobatic display performed by 'Pappy' in a then still-secret Merlin-engined Mustang. Incensed by the pilot's disregard for orders, yet stunned by his airmanship, Hill made sure that he impressed upon Herbst that he went to 'his' 23rd FG first when he showed up in the frontline in mid-1944.

Despite 'Tex' Hill's attempts to get Capt Herbst posted to the 23rd FG, the former initially served with the 5th FG(Provisional) in China, although he did not claim any victories with this group. He was eventually transferred to the 76th FS on 30 May 1944, and officially scored his first kill (a lone 'Oscar') in a P-51B on 17 June while on a weather recce mission north of Kiatow.

'Pappy' Herbst was made CO of the 74th FS on 26 June following the loss of P-40 ace, Capt J W Cruikshank (who successfully evaded with the help of the Chinese underground). Swapping Mustangs for Warhawks hardly phased a pilot of Herbst's ability, and he subsequently proceeded to score his next four kills flying a P-40N-20.

By the autumn of 1944, the Fourteenth Air Force's fighter contingent in China was proving so effective that the Japanese decided that the only way to eliminate this threat once and for all was to capture the base at Kweilin. After a bitter battle to save the airstrip, it finally fell to the enemy in September, but not before the resident Mustang and Warhawk pilots had exacted a heavy toll on Japanese aircraft supporting the offensive.

The 74th FS had converted to the P-51C-7 just prior to the assault, and on 3 September 'Pappy' Herbst scored the first Mustang victories for the unit when he led a dive-bombing attack against a railway bridge on the Hangchow-Kinwha line. Having dropped his bombs to little effect, he noticed two 'Val' dive-bombers (these were possibly Ki-51 'Sonia' recon-naissance aircraft of the 6th Sentai) appear out of the cloud below him intent on investigating the cause of the smoke that was rising from the recently attacked target. Using his height advantage to maximum effect, Herbst dived on them and quickly destroyed one of the aircraft with a single solid burst of fire.

Alerted to the danger by the explosion of his wingman, the second 'Val' pilot dived for the ground and led the Mustang on a merry chase across the paddy fields below. The Japanese pilot seemed to be trying to make Herbst either stall into the ground or fly into range of the his rear gunner, and in the end the American shot part of the aircraft's rudder off, which forced his hapless foe to attempt a crash-landing. However, as soon as the 'Val's' spatted undercarriage touched the soggy ground, the aircraft nosed over and came to rest on its back. Herbst then strafed the steaming enemy aircraft for good measure!

During the doomed defence of Kweilin, 'Pappy' Herbst accounted for a further two Japanese fighters , taking his score to nine confirmed victories by 16 September. Five of these had been scored in the P-51, which made him one of the first Mustang aces in China.

In mid-October the CO of the 118th TRS commenced a ten-week-long scoring run that would see him pip 'Pappy' Herbst to the title of top Mustang ace of the Fourteenth Air Force by a solitary victory. Maj Edward McComas had joined the 118th in early 1943 after serving for almost two years as an instructor. With a wealth of flying experience behind him, and a proven ability to teach fellow pilots the intricacies of handling a combat aircraft, McComas proved to be the natural choice to assume command of the unit in late September 1943 when its previous boss was killed in a flying accident at Key Field, Mississippi. The 118th had been redesignated a tactical recce squadron just prior to losing its CO, and McComas was left with the task of preparing the unit for its eventual overseas posting.

Equipped with P-40s, the 118th was initially sent to the Tenth Air Force in India in January 1944, where it saw little action. However, in June it moved to China to become part of the 23rd FG. In the weeks following its arrival, several pilots achieved scores in the Mustang, but not McComas, who was itching for the opportunity to prove his ability against the enemy in aerial combat. When his chance finally came on 16 October he took it with both hands.

Lt Col Edward O McComas stands by his P-51C near the end of his tour in January 1945. Curiously, this aircraft has been adorned with 19 Japanese flags, although its pilot's overall score totalled 14 destroyed, one damaged and one probable

On this day McComas had led a flight of 118th TRS Mustangs on an armed recce of Hong Kong's Victoria Harbour, where his charges had encountered a formation of Ki-44 'Tojos'. The squadron boss soon despatched one of the fighters into the harbour and damaged a second, before breaking off the engagement and returning to Luliang.

Having tasted success, McComas was eager to seek out more targets, although the enemy was becoming increasingly more difficult to find in the air. Known for being a hard taskmaster who would settle for nothing less than 100 per cent commitment from his pilots when in the air (a trait which led to him being less than popular with some members of his squadron), McComas nevertheless demanded as much from himself. He soon proved this by downing a second 'Tojo' and three 'Oscars' by 19 December, thus securing his place as the 118th TRS's second ace.

A further two kills fell to the guns of McComas's P-51C 48 hours later, but his big day was to come on 23 December. His unit had specialised in skip-bombing Japanese shipping along the Chinese coast upon their arrival in-theatre, and had achieved notable successes since the summer. On this day, McComas was leading a formation of 16 Mustangs that had been briefed to attack Hankow-Wuchang ferry installations, and upon arriving over the target, the aircraft split into two eight-ship flights. Whilst the first section attacked the target, McComas patrolled above the diving P-51s with the remaining seven aircraft, providing fighter cover.

Once he had thoroughly checked that there were no enemy fighters in the area, he led his charges on a strafing attack on nearby Huchang airfield. After destroying a Ki-48 and damaging a Ki-43 on the ground, McComas decided to head for home, but just as he started to climb away from the airfield, he spotted a formation of six 'Oscars' flying above him. One of the Japanese fighters attacked him from astern and scored hits on the Mustang's wing before McComas could dive away out of range.

Climbing up to 7000 ft, the American pilot chased down a lone 'Oscar'

This P-51C of the 23rd FG is equipped with underwing M-10 rocket tubes, which proved to be less successful than the zero-length stubs also used in-theatre (see the photo on page 51 for an example of the latter weapon) (*Hess*)

and pressed home his attack until its pilot abandoned the damaged fighter. This prompted a savage response from two of the downed Ki-43 pilot's comrades, who forced McComas to head south-east over the Japanese airbase at Ehur Tao Kow, near Kiukiang. Having shaken off his assailants with a burst of speed, he sighted no fewer than nine 'Oscars' preparing to scramble from the airfield that he had just overflown. Such odds were even a bit much for the fighting mettle of Ed McComas, so he set about reducing them before the combat really developed .

He circled and made a perfectly timed west-to-east pass on the first two Ki-43s to clear the runway. Hitting the leading aircraft just as its pilot was retracting the gear, the 'Oscar' rolled over onto its back and collided with the second fighter. A second pair of Ki-43s then attempted to take-off in pursuit of the impudent American Mustang, but they only succeeded in giving McComas the opportunity to line up behind them and shoot each of them down from very close range. With little ammunition left, the 'ace in a day' turned for home.

Few pilots achieved five kills in a single sortie in China, and Lt Col Ed McComas was the only one to do it in a Mustang. Just for good measure, he scored a solitary kill (yet another 'Oscar') over Hong Kong the following day to register his 14th, and last, victory.

Late CBI P-51 Aces

By the autumn of 1944 all four units within the 23rd FG had at last become fully equipped with the Mustang. Other squadrons from the 51st FG and the 311th FG (the latter having been re-rolled from a dive-bombing outfit, equipped with A-36s, into a fighter group with the arrival of P-51Bs in May 1944) had also received examples of the North American Aviation fighter by this late stage in the war, thus making the P-51 the dominant American type in China.

The Packard Merlin Mustang's range was one of its great assets, and it was exploited to the full by the 23rd FG's 74th FS on the afternoon of 3 November 1944 when the unit mounted a long-range mission on Amoy, situated across the straits off Formosa. Participating in this sweep were Lt John Bolyard and Capt Paul Reis, who were searching the shipping lanes for Japanese vessels when they spotted two 'Zekes' preparing to land after protecting a convoy that was entering Amoy Harbour. Reis immediately went for the lead fighter, while Bolyard concentrated on the wingman.

As chance would have it, the lead Zero was flown by 32-victory ace, Warrant Officer Takeo Tanimizu (see *Osprey Aircraft of the Aces 22 - Imperial Japanese Navy Aces 1937-45* for details). Reis opened fire at extreme range, but had only succeeded in inflicting incidental damage to his target's wingtip. Tanimizu actually thought that his inexperienced wingman, Manubo Ito, had accidentally fired shots at him as they had come into land!

Meanwhile, Bolyard had slipped in below the now alerted wingman and delivered a deadly blow from 500 yards that resulted in the enemy fighter exploding in mid-air. Realising the grave predicament now facing him, Tanimizu tried to raise his flaps and landing gear in an effort to climb away and take the fight to the Americans. However, Bolyard had spotted him and used his speed advantage to close on the wallowing 'Zeke' and set its fuel tanks alight with an accurate burst of fire.

Tanimizu managed to free himself from his doomed fighter just in time to have his parachute open a few feet above Amoy Harbour. Bolyard had gained the first of his five victories, and Tanimizu was plucked out the water burned and dazed from his first encounter with the P-51 in China.

Another in the sequence of long-range missions deep into eastern China was flown on 10 November when a radar site at Yochow was hit by elements of the 75th FS, while a second flight from the same unit flew fighter cover overhead. A total of 12 P-51Cs were involved in the sortie, with the covering flight led by veteran Canadian-born pilot, Capt Forrest Parham. The latter was soon in action when seven 'Oscars' appeared over the radar site in an attempt to disrupt the American attack, and one of the two Ki-43s shot down during the subsequent melee was credited to Parham for his first Mustang and fourth overall victory – he had downed three aircraft flying P-40Ns earlier in the year.

The following day 16 75th FS Mustangs made a long-range fighter sweep down the Hsiang river valley, where they were jumped by enemy fighters. Three Mustangs were quickly lost, but other P-51s chased the Japanese off the tails of their comrades. Amongst those pilots to claim kills in this bloody action was Forrest Parham, who scored his fifth, and last, victory (a 'Hamp') and damaged a further two fighters ('Oscars'). Brooklyn-born Lt Don Lopez also 'made ace' on this sortie with his final kill of the campaign. Attacking one of the first Ki-84 'Frank' fighters seen in-theatre, Lopez was frustrated when his four .50-cal guns jammed and the Nakajima fighter escaped. However, he had earlier despatched an 'Oscar' for his fifth kill – all his claims were against Ki-43s, four of which had been destroyed flying P-40Ns between December 1943 and August 1944. Although this action had been a costly one for the 75th FS, Don Lopez had been fortunate to be on it for it was his last day of operations prior to going home on rotation.

As the final unit within the 23rd FG to convert onto the P-51C, the pilots of the 75th were more than a

P-51D-10 44-14626 was used for a very short time by Lt Col Ed McComas prior to him returning to the USA in January 1945 (*Hess*)

This 2nd ACG P-51D-15 came to grief whilst landing on 17 February 1945. Note the distinctive fuselage lightning bolt and exclamation mark on the fin. Judging by the lack of exhaust staining on the nose of the Mustang, the aircraft had only just arrived in India when it suffered this minor mishap (*Mayer via Crow*)

Devoid of a serial number, this rocket-toting P-51D nevertheless sports the 2nd ACG's lightning bolt marking. When fitted with external tanks, the group's Mustangs could range as far as south-western China during patrols from their Kalaikunda base (*Hess*)

little reluctant to part with their trusty Warhawks, which had formed their equipment since 1942. Lopez preferred the P-40 for strafing and aerial combat, noting that the original installation of the wing guns on the Mustang promised jamming in anything but perfectly straight and level firing. The coolant lines that seemed to run for miles within the Mustang's fuselage were also a constant worry, since a single hit could render the liquid-cooled Packard Merlin unusable within two or three minutes. In comparison with the P-40N, the Mustang was much faster, longer ranging and more manoeuvrable at speeds above 300 mph, but it never supplanted the Warhawk in the affections of the 75th's pilots in the few remaining months of the war

That is not to say, however, that the Mustang was not without its champions within the squadron, one of whom was Lt Wiltz 'Flash' Segura. Although he had scored all six of his victories in the P-40M/N by September 1944 (just prior to the unit's conversion onto the Mustang), his memory of the P-51 is most affirmative;

'The Mustang was a breath of fresh air compared to the P-40. It could out-climb, out-dive, out-run and out-shoot the Jap Zero. The only thing it could not do was out-turn the Zero – I don't think any aeroplane could turn with the Zero. Prior to the arrival of the P-51, we fought a defensive fight, but with the advent of the P-51 it became an offensive fight.

'I flew the P-51 a lot after World War 2, as well as the P-47 and P-38. They were all good aeroplanes, but none were as good as the P-51. The '51, in my estimation, was the best prop fighter of the war.'

The Mustang's 'long legs' were amply demonstrated yet again on 8 December when the 74th FS sent 16 aircraft to attack the old Chinese capital of Nanking. 'Pappy' Herbst wanted to remind the Japanese of the Pearl Harbor anniversary (China was a day ahead of Hawaii because of its position west of the International Date Line) by making a strong raid with his newly-organised 'guerrilla' force.

Things went well on the mission, especially during the initial stages when eight bomb-carrying Mustangs successfully attacked vessels moored along a river near to the city – two 'Oscars' that tried to interfere with the bombing were also quickly shot down. Flushed with these victories, the Mustang pilots proceeded to attack airfields in the surrounding area, claiming a further 18 Japanese aircraft destroyed on the ground.

Although more army fighters had tried to interfere with the strafing attacks, they fared no better than the first pair of 'Oscars' the 74th FS had encountered. Lt John Bolyard was in one of the Mustangs performing top cover for the strafers, and he went 'head-to-head' with an attacking Ki-61 on several occasions before the Japanese fighter finally fell to the Mustang's fire from an altitude of about 4000 ft. Bolyard then sighted a solitary Ki-44 and slipped in behind it without alerting its seemingly oblivious pilot. Carefully taking aim, the American fired a short burst at close range and the fighter crashed in flames. These two kills now took John Bolyard's score to four.

Ten days later, the Fourteenth Air Force enjoyed one of its most successful days with the Mustang, operations on this date also ushering in the last good period of scoring for the Americans in China. The 74th FS was led on this day by future CO, Maj Phil Chapman, with 'Pappy' Herbst coming along 'for the ride' to oversee the performance of his successor. Striking at airfields around the Hankow area, the latter pilot claimed an 'Oscar' for his 11th victory (and his first kill in almost two months), while three other Ki-43s were destroyed around the target area – one of these was credited to Phil Chapman, who downed the 'Oscar' over Wuchang satellite airfield for his first in a total of five kills.

Newly-promoted Deputy Commander of the 23rd FG, Lt Col Charles Older, was also involved in this mission, tagging along with Ed McComas's 118th TRS. An extremely experienced fighter pilot who had scored ten kills with the original 'Flying Tigers' in 1941-42, Older had returned to China in July 1944 to serve with the 23rd FG's HQ flight. He had claimed a kill in a 76th FS P-51B within weeks of his arrival back in the frontline, but had subsequently found the enemy incredibly elusive. He had no such trouble on 18 December, however, attacking an 'Oscar' near the Wuchang airstrip. The enemy fighter took hits in the fuselage and wing, and was seen to crash by Older's wingman.

The following day 'Chuck' Older confirmed that he still had what it took to be a frontline fighter pilot when he claimed a 'Lily' bomber and a further two Ki-43s in the same area during a lone early morning patrol to the Hankow area. He initially stalked and shot down the Ki-48 near one of the region's many airfield's, before strafing yet another airstrip from which four 'Oscars' took off to engage him in combat. Older needed to show little skill, however, to descend on the Ki-43s as they strained for

This near-planform view of P-51D-15 44-15450 reveals that the 2nd ACG also applied 'bolts to the upper wing surfaces of its Mustangs

altitude, and he shot one down on his first attacking pass before fleeing the scene. He was later jumped by about 12 more 'Oscars' whilst returning to base, but managed to outfly them thanks to the overwhelming superiority of his mount – he even added another kill to his tally in the process. Older's behaviour showed a confidence in his Mustang that perhaps wouldn't have been so evident with the old P-40 Warhawk.

Lt Col Older repeated his triple haul in the New Year when he downed a 'Betty', a 'Sonia' and a 'Tess' on a sweep of Tachang

airfield on 17 January. This took Older's final score to 18, making him one of the CBI's leading aces.

Returning to 18 December, Capt Floyd Finberg of the 74th FS participated in an attack on an airfield at Kiukiang which saw his unit destroy no fewer than ten aircraft on the ground. Finberg was credited with six of these, which represented slightly more than half of the total ground victories he would claim by war's end. He was also credited with a solitary aerial victory, plus others probably destroyed or damaged. Like the Eighth Air Force, the rules for air combat claims in the CBI at the time gave ground kills equal billing with aerial successes, meaning that Finberg's impressive combined tally of 12 victories (11 of which were scored on the ground) made him a CBI Mustang ace.

The raid on 18 December had also seen pilots of the 311th FG get among the victories whilst escorting B-25s to targets in the Hankow area. Leading group ace, and 530th FS boss, Maj James England, accounted for one 'Oscar' (this was his last kill of the war, taking his final tally to ten), whilst fellow squadron pilot, Lt Lester Arasmith, claimed two more Ki-43s and a 'Tojo' to increase his score to four.

The 18th will always be remembered as a great day for the Mustang in a forgotten theatre. More than 20 Japanese fighters had been claimed in

*The 75th FS received its first P-51Ds in early 1945, but due to the paucity of aerial opposition its pilots had little chance of proving the fighter's aerial supremacy on the China front (**Michael O'Leary**)*

A pair of 530th FS P-51Ds fly close escort for a C-47 over China on 24 August 1945 (*Michael O'Leary*)

the air and a similar number destroyed on the ground, for the loss of three P-51s reported as missing. A further 40 claims had been made by Mustang pilots before year end.

Early in 1945 the last of the CBI Mustang aces rounded out their scores, with Lester Arasmith claiming an 'Oscar' over Sinsiang airfield on 5 January to 'make ace', and squadronmate Lt Leonard Reeves accounting for a further three Nakajima fighters on the same mission to take his tally to four. Both pilots would claim their final victories when the 530th FS downed a number of 'Oscars' and 'Tojos' in the Nanking area in late March.

'Pappy' Herbst also completed his remarkable run with three kills in a little over 24 hours on 16/17 January, his trusty P-51B-7 ranging far and wide in a series of sorties that saw him down a G3M 'Nell' bomber north of Formosa, a 'Tess' (almost certainly an L2D 'Tabby') south of Yuhwan and a 'Tojo' between Tachang and Kiangwan airfields. The ranking ace of the CBI, Herbst's final tally was 18 destroyed, one probable and three damaged.

The two little-publicised Chinese-American Composite Wings had also begun to re-equip with P-51s by early 1945, and although the majority of their kills were scored with the venerable P-40N, two of the six aces produced by the 3rd FG(P) scored their final victories with the Mustang. Ranking ace Lt Heyward Paxton (of the 7th FS(P)) claimed three of his 6.5 kills with the P-51C in the first fortnight of 1945, although he was shot down soon after scoring his final victory on 14 January – despite being injured, he successfully evaded. Squadronmate Capt Kuang-Fu Wang (a veteran of the pre-war Chinese Air Force) claimed the last of his 6.5 kills whilst still part of the Fourteenth Air Force in a P-51K on 7 March. Made joint CO (each squadron had a Chinese and American commanding officer) of the 7th FS(P) soon afterwards, he reportedly downed a further two aircraft before VJ-Day, although they have never been officially recognised.

Another 7th FS(P) pilot claimed the unique honour of having scored more ground kills than any other pilot in the USAAF, period. Capt Thomas Reynolds was already a ground victory ace with the P-40 when he was made joint CO of the unit in late 1944, and over the next few weeks he shot down a further three 'Tojos' and destroyed an estimated 25 Japanese aircraft on the ground – ten of these came in a single sortie to one of the airfields at Tsingtao on 10 February. This haul, combined with his numerous successes whilst flying Warhawks, gave Thomas Reynolds an overall tally of four aerial victories and no fewer than 31.5 ground kills!

P-51K-1 44-11447 *SHADY KATY* was part of the 311th FG's postwar complement of Mustangs, and it was photographed in India on 23 November 1945 (*Michael O'Leary*)

CENTRAL PACIFIC

The last organisation to use both the P-47 and P-51 against the Japanese in the Pacific was the Seventh Air Force. Having the distinction of being in continuous combat from Pearl Harbor through to VJ-Day, the air force's VII Fighter Command was also unique in controlling units that were solely equipped with P-51Ds and P-47Ns from mid-1944 through to war's end.

Before getting into the 'nuts and bolts' details of who did what in the Central Pacific, a few points explaining the assignment of individual groups within this theatre is relevant. The USAAF adopted a complicated system of control for its fighter units in the Central Pacific during the final months of the war, the 15th, 21st and 506th FGs being assigned to the Seventh Air Force's subordinate VII FC, while the 318th, 413th, 414th and 508th were technically controlled by the Twentieth Air Force. However, missions for the latter quartet of groups were assigned by VII FC, and groups from both air forces regularly flew alongside each other whilst escorting B-29s over Japan!

Finally, the 507th FG was also part of the Twentieth Air Force right up until 14 August 1945, when it was assigned to the newly-arrived Eighth Air Force, fresh in the Pacific from its victorious tour of duty in the ETO – all other VII FC groups were also assigned to the 'Mighty Eighth' soon after VJ-Day.

Returning to the Seventh Air Force, this organisation had grown out of the old pre-war Hawaiian Air Force in February 1942. For the next two-and-a-half years its fighter groups flew firstly Curtiss P-36 and then P-40 fighters, as well as a small number of P-39 Airacobras and older model

This impressive photograph shows a formation of 15th FG P-51Ds cruising at altitude over the Pacific during one of the first VLR bombing missions flown to Japan in April 1945 (*IWM via Hess*)

One of the pilots who tasted success during the first missions over the Japanese homeland was six-kill ace Maj Harry Crim of the 531st FS/21st FG

P-38s. Little action was seen during this time, although several individual squadrons were briefly involved in the campaign to retake the Marshall Islands in 1943-44, and the 318th FG was employed in the ground-attack role on Saipan from mid-1944 onwards.

It was only when the USAAF's long-range bombing campaign got into full swing from Iwo Jima in early 1945 that the fighter groups of the Seventh Air Force (re-equipped with the latest Mustang and Thunderbolt variants in late 1944) had the opportunity to at last take the fight to the enemy in the air. It therefore comes as little surprise to find that all ten pilots that 'made ace' whilst flying with the Seventh did so in the final months of the war.

One of the first fighter group within VII FC to receive the P-47 was the 318th FG, which replaced its complement of P-40Ns with new Thunderbolts whilst still Hawaii-based. Forward deployed to Saipan as part of the Marianas Islands' invasion force in June 1944, the group actually arrived in-theatre courtesy of two US Navy aircraft carriers – no fewer than 73 P-47Ds had been flown from the decks of the 'flat tops' into the recently-liberated Aslito Field by 26 June.

The men of the 318th had barely taken in their surroundings when they were subjected to a nocturnal raid on the base by Japanese ground forces at daybreak the following morning. Swapping Thunderbolts for side-arms, the men of the group acquitted themselves well in the bloody infantry action which followed, and succeeded in limiting the damage to a solitary P-47 destroyed. This desperate attack by the Japanese was meant to deal the 318th a killer blow by knocking out as many of the newly-arrived fighters as possible. However, they failed miserably, and the Thunderbolt pilots started flying ground support missions almost as soon as they had landed on the embattled island.

Later that same summer the last of the islands in the Marianas chain fell to American forces, giving the 318th FG more opportunity to oppose the Japanese aircraft operating from bases on Okinawa and other Home Islands. Leading ace of the group's 19th FS was Lt Stanley Lustic, who scored the first of his six kills on an early offensive sweep from Saipan on 27 November 1944. The group was credited with eight victories, Lustic claiming a 'Zeke' whilst flying a P-47D.

Aerial victories were few and far between for the group during this time as the short-ranged D-model Thunderbolt was restricted to flying local operations over the Central Pacific, which had been 'cleansed' of all aerial opposition within weeks of the invasion. In a desperate measure to seek out the enemy, a handful of longer-ranged P-38Ls were supplied to the 318th in November 1944, and several escort missions to Volcano and Truk Islands, and Iwo Jima, were subsequently flown, but precious few encounters with enemy aircraft were recorded.

One pilot who did, however, enjoy some success with the Lightning was the 318th FG's ranking ace, the formidably-named Capt Judge Wolfe of the 333rd FS. A pilot with the group from 1942 through to 1945 (he spent eight months recuperating from injuries suffered in a forced-landing in a P-47 between April 1944 and January 1945), Wolfe was on yet another mission to Iwo Jima on 10 February 1945 when he spotted two G4M 'Betty' bombers climbing through cloud below him. He immediately pulled in behind the two unescorted aircraft and

Maj James Tapp of the 78th FS/15th FG scored eight kills over Japan in April/May 1945 – many of them in this P-51D-20 (44-63984)

clinically despatched both bombers with the minimum of fuss – these two kills were amongst the few victories scored by the P-38 in the Central Pacific. Seven more Japanese fighters would fall to Wolfe's guns in May/June following the 318th's re-equipment with the awesome P-47N – including a haul of four kills (two 'Zekes' and two 'Jacks') on 10 June north of Kagoshima Wan.

The first long-range N-model Thunderbolts had arrived on Saipan in March 1945, and on the last day of the following month, the 318th moved to the small island of Ie Shima, off the north-western coast of Okinawa. The move of the group ever closer to Japan had also coincided with the arrival on Iwo Jima of the Mustang-equipped 15th and 21st FGs from bases in Hawaii.

A handful of introductory missions to fairly distant targets, as well as ground support sorties for the Marines slogging their way across Iwo Jima, followed their arrival in the frontline. The latter, in particular, must have had some effect on the enemy, for a surprise raid was made on the Central Field camp on the night of 26/27 March by 300 Japanese troops which saw the 21st FG's dispersal temporarily overrun and 11 pilots killed or wounded (including the CO of the 531st FS).

Despite this temporary reversal, the 21st FG was able to take its place alongside the 15th FG on 7 April as both groups participated in the first Very-Long-Range (VLR) mission to the Japanese mainland. No fewer than 106 P-51Ds were despatched as escorts for B-29 Superfortresses sent to bomb the Nakajima engine works in Tokyo. This mission was of a far greater duration than anything that had been previously attempted by VII FC squadrons in a single-engined fighter, and many of the pilots involved in the raid were understandably apprehensive about this. Uncertainties about the weather and Japanese reaction to the attack also played on the minds of the pilots, but in the event, their fears were largely unjustified.

Weather along the route proved to be reasonably benign, and the Japanese defences had apparently set themselves to attack the USAAF formation at an altitude much higher than the bomber's cruising height of just 18,000 ft – Mustang pilots could see the contrails of interceptors high above.

One of those individuals looking up at those contrails was veteran fighter pilot Maj Jim Tapp, who, like many of the men serving with VII FC units, had been a part of the 15th FG's 78th FS for over two years, and had effectively been 'kicking his heels' along with the rest of the command's pilots in Hawaii since mid-1942. Whilst keeping tabs on the enemy above him, he also spared a few seconds to look down on the stunning sight of a snow-covered Mt Fuji as it slipped past below the large formation, which continued to head for Tokyo.

Having tracked the USAAF force for a number of minutes, the Japanese interceptors finally decided to press home their attack, prompting Tapp into immediate action. Flying P-51D-10 44-63984 (which he used for all eight of his kills), he soon had a twin-engined Ki-45 'Nick' square in his sights, and from a distance of 400 yards, closed to near-collision with his guns blazing. Exhilarated by at last seeing some action after so many fruitless patrols over the wide expanses of the Central Pacific, James Tapp was not too concerned about confirming whether his victim crashed or not, so he mentally registered it as a probable – it was later upgraded to confirmed. His remaining three kills over the next few minutes left him with little doubt as to their final fate, however, as he noted some years after the war;

'As I pulled to return to my previous escort position, I saw a "Tony" painted (olive drab) coming down on an attack. This time I decided to go after him a little slower. I closed on him from his left side, about 15° off his tail. I started firing at about a 1000 ft and immediately got hits, but this time I had a flamer. As I passed him on his left side at very close range, I could

This P-47N of the 333rd FS/318th FG boasted one of the more risque pieces of nose art to be found on Ie Shima in 1945. Its nickname referred both to the aircraft and the artwork!

see the pilot sitting in the cockpit, which was aflame. Bob Carr, the number four man in my flight, saw the pilot bail out and took a picture of him with his gun camera.

'As we pulled up off the "Tony", I saw a "Dinah" which appeared to be initiating a head-on attack. We had been told by our intelligence officer that it (had) been reported that "Dinahs" had been making frontal rocket and phosphorus bomb attacks on bomber formations. The activity with the "Nick" and "Tony" had brought us down to a lower altitude. Not being able to trade altitude for speed to the extent that I had on the other two, I "poured on the coals" in order to close on the "Dinah".

'As we went diving down through about 18,000 ft, the P-51's engine automatically switched to low blower, which seemed to stop us in mid-air – the P-51 had an automatic high blower system, which meant that as you climbed to altitude, a pressure-sensing switch at the carburettor intake would cause the blower to shift to high between 16,000 and 18,000 ft, depending on the ram air pressure. I saw that I wasn't going to close, so I attempted a shot from out of range. The attack had started from his front quarter, and at this point I was at the 90° point. I had to fly almost 90° bank to develop a big lead, since the "Dinah" was going quite fast. As a

These two P-51D-20s were assigned to the 48th FS/21st FG, and were photographed escorting B-29s to Japan (*Ron Witt via Jim Crow*)

consequence, the target became blanked out by the nose of my P-51. A few incendiary strikes were noted, but I had no confidence that I did any good.

'I then saw an unpainted "Oscar" getting set to go after somebody. I started a 90° full deflection curve of pursuit pass. I started firing at 1000 ft and 90°, and continued on around to very close range off his tail. I got hits all through the pass, and observed pieces coming off the "Oscar", but he never caught fire.

Yet another escort shot, this P-51D-20 wears the markings of the 47th FS/15th FG, as well as bearing the nickname *Squirt* beneath its exhaust stubs

The "Oscar" rolled into a steep descending spiral. Phil Maher observed the "Oscar" continue the spiral descent into the ground.

'As I pulled up off the "Oscar", I saw six Jap aircraft coming straight at us. As I faced them, those to my left were in a four-ship formation and appeared to be "Zekes" (Zeros). On the right was a two-ship formation of something else. Initially I thought they were "Tojos", but have since concluded that they must have been N1K "Georges", or some variant. What would two Army "Tojos" be doing with four Navy "Zekes"? I picked the one on the right to go head-on with. I started firing at about 1500 ft or so. This pass of course would be only a few seconds long. I observed flashes on the bogey's engine, fuselage and left wing. I thought at first the latter was his 20 mm firing back. I was a little puzzled because they were too far out on the wing. As soon as we passed, the Japs made a hard left turn, while I started a slow high speed climbing turn.'

Maher also saw this fighter going down with part of its left wing missing, and reported to the pugnacious Tapp that fuel was low. Tapp was ready to take on the five remaining Japanese fighters, but elected to return to the rally point in accordance with mission policy in respect to fuel levels. Maj Tapp was eventually credited with four victories on his first combat, and would later become the first ace of the Seventh Air Force.

The 21st FG also did well on this initial escort to Japan, claiming five Japanese fighters destroyed. Total American losses amounted to three B-29s, one P-51 lost to flak and another ditched, with its pilot rescued by a US Navy destroyer. The 531st FS's CO of just 12 days, Capt Harry Crim, was credited with two of these victories, claiming a 'Tony' and a 'Nick' – he would end the war as the ranking squadron ace with six kills.

A veteran of a Mediterranean tour on P-38s with the 14th FG in 1943 (he had led the 37th FS towards the end of his time in the MTO), Harry Crim had joined the 21st FG's 72nd FS as Ops Officer in August 1944. He had been hastily transferred to the 531st FS after its CO, Maj J H Hudson, had been wounded in the surprise raid on Central Field camp on Iwo Jima on the night of 26/27 March 1945.

Although of average quality, this photo is a rare view of a 464th FS P-47N commencing a VLR mission almost certainly from Ie Shima in the spring of 1945. Depending on the target for the day, the pilot could expect to endure a further eight hours in the cockpit of his Thunderbolt before recovering back at base

Having flown most of the USAAF frontline fighter types either in action or as an instructor, Harry Crim was well placed to compare the various types. He was enthusiastic about each one, considering it his good fortune to have flown two of the finest fighters in the US Army inventory (P-38 and P-51). Crim observed that although the P-38 would have had some psychological reassurance for a pilot

involved in long over-water escorts thanks to the redundancy offered by its second engine, the Packard Merlin in the Mustang provided few misgivings in service.

Maj Crim also came to quickly appreciate the value of maintaining a combat formation with his Mustang flight over Japan once the enemy was engaged, and expressed the opinion that even with the aircraft's sterling fighting qualities, it was foolhardy to remain in the combat area without a wingman.

OKINAWAN P-47s

The 318th FG was joined by the recently-formed (October 1944) 507th and 413th FGs during May and June 1945, both groups having been specifically created for VLR operations from bases in the Pacific. However, following their arrival at Ie Shima in May 1945, they found themselves initially tasked with flying ground-support missions for troops slogging it out in bitter hand-to-hand fighting with the remnants of the Japanese Army on Okinawa. It was only after the last pockets of resistance had been 'mopped up' that both groups joined the 318th FG on VLR escort missions – the first of these was flown in late May.

As the most experienced P-47 group in-theatre, it fell to the 318th to score the bulk of the kills credited to the P-47N. Indeed, its pilots proved well-suited to the escort role, downing 48 enemy aircraft in a single week in late May for the loss of just three Thunderbolts.

Two missions in particular yielded great success, the 318th FG revelling in the rare freedom of flying over Japan without having to escort B-29s. On 25 May, the group carried out a series of wide-ranging sweeps of the area around southern Kyushu, with the 19th FS, in particular, exacting a heavy toll on the enemy. More than 20 Japanese aircraft were credited to the unit as having been shot down in a frenetic sequence of intercepts against *kamikazes* intent on hitting naval targets sailing in the waters between Kyushu and Okinawa.

Lts Richard Anderson and Leon Cox found themselves in the thick of the action when they bounced a large group of 'Zekes' off Amami O Shima. The latter pilot was credited with three victories, whilst Anderson went two better to become the Seventh Air Force's first 'ace-in-a-day' – these proved to be his only kills of the conflict. Lt Stanley Lustic also added three 'Oscars' to his solitary kill from the previous November, having engaged the trio of fighters about 50 miles northwest of Okinawa.

The second day of heavy scoring came just 72 hours later when 17 more *kamikazes* were destroyed en route to their intended targets. Capt John Vogt became the second 19th FS 'ace-in-a-day' when he led his flight into a formation of 30 'Zekes' off the coast of Kyushu. He managed to down five of the Japanese fighters during the course of the engagement, whilst a sixth was credited to him as a probable. Stanley Lustic was also among the kills again, claiming two Mitsubishi fighters to take his final tally to six.

The 318th FG's sole remaining ace also scored his first victories on this date, Lt William Mathis (of the 19th FS) downing three 'Zekes' that he had encountered during a sweep over an airfield at Kanoya. He would destroy a further two 'Zekes' off Kikai Shima on the morning of 22 June, thus becoming the final ace of his group.

The 333rd FS was also active on 28 May, downing three *kamikazes* off the Okinawan coast. One of these was credited to Judge Wolfe, who would go on to score an additional six kills in the P-47N by 10 June.

ACES OVER JAPAN

Like the 318th on Ie Shima, both the 15th and 21st FGs on Iwo Jima were reinforced in April 1945 by a recently-formed P-47N group in the shape of the 506th FG. Immediately tasked with escorting B-29s on day raids to Japan, the new group continued with this routine until a decision was made soon after its arrival to switch the Superfortresses to the night bombing mission, thus rendering escorts redundant, and giving fighter pilots more freedom to undertake group-generated sweeps over Japan. This tactical decision had an immediate (and positive) effect on the fortunes of VII FC pilots, who made the most of the chance to fight over Japan free of the bombers.

For the remainder of April 1945 the Iwo Jima-based Mustang pilots did well on both escort missions and free sweeps, claiming nearly 50 victories for the loss of 17 P-51s. Two of the kills claimed during the month fell to Maj Jim Tapp, thus taking him past the magical 'five', and making him the first ace of not only the 15th FG, but also the Seventh Air Force;

'After a few days of celebrating my four kills on the 7th, we were at it again on 12 April. This time we had some of the younger pilots along, but we also had other problems as well. Again it was an escort mission to Tokyo. We got to the rendezvous point far ahead to the strike aircraft, which messed up our fuel management. The air was full of smoke which limited our visibility. On the way in I never saw any aircraft that I could go after.

'On the escort leg after the target, I got my only action. I spotted another "Tony" and came up on his tail, (and) in a pretty good turn, I quickly set this one on fire, too. This made it five aerial victories. Unfortunately, my wingman, Lt Fred White, crossed over underneath me as I was firing at the "Tony". He had some shell casings go into his airscoop which apparently punctured his radiator. About the time we crossed the coast, heading for the rally point, the element leader noticed a fine mist coming out of his aircraft. We decided to try to make it home hoping that it was the intercooler side of the system that was leaking.

'I flew his wing so that if something happened I could stay with him. As we neared the Lifeguard submarine and Superdumbo at the halfway point, his engine puffed smoke from its exhaust stacks and quit. He had anticipated having to bail out so was set to do so. After he released the canopy (he) seemed to slump forward in the cockpit. He then sat up and quickly rolled over and dropped out of the airplane. Although we had a lot of eyes looking, he was not spotted. We made a wide circle, but being tight on fuel we headed for home. We had made contact with Superdumbo, which also searched the area, but found nothing.'

These dangerously long missions over many miles of open sea exacted a fearful toll on the Mustang squadrons. Even minor battle damage caused great concern to pilots nursing their aircraft over hundreds of miles of water for several hours. The weather along the route was also daunting, as evinced by a mission to Osaka in which 27 Mustangs out of a force of 148 went down in heavy frontal weather. Two of the pilots were

This quartet of 45th FS/15th FG P-51D-20s all boast identical nose art, with individual names sprayed forward of the unit badge. They were photographed during a B-29 escort mission in mid 1945 (*Michael O'Leary*)

eventually rescued, but the others simply disappeared. However, 27 surviving Mustangs broke through the front into clear weather and continued the sortie, protecting the bombers and claiming one Japanese aircraft. This particular mission gave a telling indication of the spirit imbued in the pilots serving with the Mustang groups.

One individual who undoubtedly had these required fighting qualities in abundance was Maj Robert 'Todd' Moore, the Seventh Air Force's ranking ace. Having scored a rare kill in a P-40N with the 45th FS/15th FG in early 1944 during a long-range interception over Arno Atoll, in the Marshall Islands, Moore then had to wait until April 1945 to add to his tally. By then he had returned to the 78th FS (he had originally been posted to this unit when first sent to the 15th FG in early 1943), which had begun flying Long Range Empire Missions (a 1600-mile round trip) from Iwo Jima in P-51D-20s.

Moore participated in the very first VLR, flown on 7 April, and marked the occasion by destroying two 'Hamps' over Choshi Point, near Tokyo. He followed this up with an 'Oscar' kill 15 days later on VLR mission number five, and then 'made ace' on 25 May when he downed two 'Zekes' over Kashiwa airfield. Moore then transferred back to the 45th FS, and on his first combat sortie with the unit 'second time round' (on 28 May), he experienced his greatest day in combat.

Part of an escort numbering 101 Mustangs sortied to protect 400 B-29s attacking the port city of Yokohama, Moore (in P-51D-20 44-63483) quickly realised that he was in for the fight of his life as one of the largest formations of enemy interceptors ever encountered on a VLR flew headlong into the bombers as they approached the navy's Atsugi airfield. Moore's flight was providing the escort for the leading formation of Superfortresses, and duly bore the brunt of the initial assault. Fixing his sights on a flight of three 'Jacks', the Mustang ace downed his opposite number with a textbook example of deflection shooting, then claimed the number two J2M with a solitary burst of fire after a short chase. Reforming his flight, Moore then returned to station above the B-29s.

Fifteen minutes later, when directly over Yokohama, Moore spotted a pair of 'Georges' away to his right that were shaping up to dive on the B-29s below, so he immediately bounced them. Although one got away, the second fighter pulled into the now rapidly closing Mustang pilot and opened fire. However, Moore's marksmanship was better, and he ripped the N1K2-J apart with two well-aimed bursts. Having downed three examples of the latest navy fighters in a little over 15 minutes, 'Todd' Moore was now the 15th FG's leading ace – a position he was not to relinquish.

Another Mustang pilot to enjoy success on 29 May was 531st FS boss Maj Harry Crim, who doubled his score by claiming a pair of 'Zekes' destroyed (and a third damaged) off Chiba Peninsular, south of Tokyo. His fifth kill (a 'Betty') followed on 1 July during a VLR sweep of Hamamatsu airfield, on the east coast of Hokkaido, and his sixth, and last, five days later when he downed a 'Zeke' (and damaged a further three fighters) encountered over Sagami-wan.

Although not scoring five kills with the Mustang, distinguished fighter ace Lt Col John W Mitchell of Operation *Dillinger* fame (he had led the P-38s that shot down Adm Yamamoto's 'Betty' bomber on 18 April 1943) enjoyed some success with the P-51D as part of the 15th FG's HQ flight in June, and then briefly with the 21st FG, before returning to the 15th as its CO. Despite having not scored a kill since 2 February 1943, Mitchell soon found his touch, adding a 'Zeke' to his tally on 26 June, followed by two 'Georges' on 16 July. This took Mitchell's final wartime tally to 11, and he would later add a further four MiG-15s to his score over Korea in 1953 whilst serving as CO of the 51st FIW.

LAST VICTORIES

With the war having just weeks to run as the month of August arrived, VII FC pilots continued their now well-established routine of fighter sweeps

Two days after the atomic bombings, these 348th FG Mustangs stand neatly parked at Ie Shima waiting for a mission in a war that had come to a sudden, and startling, conclusion (*Michael O'Leary*)

over the Home Islands. One of the more significant victories claimed during this final month of global conflict fell to the boss of the 413th FG's 34th FS, Lt Col Carl Payne. CO of the P-47N-equipped unit since its formation on 24 October 1944, Payne had led his men into Ie Shima as recently as 14 June, which left the 34th FS with little opportunity to make a real impression in the Central Pacific. Indeed, the unit scored just three kills up to VJ-Day, although one of these fell to the CO when he destroyed a 'Zeke' over Yawata, near Kyushu, on 8 August. This was his sixth, and last, kill of the war, having earlier 'made ace' flying Spitfires with the 309th FS/31st FG in the MTO in 1942-43.

Two days later VII FC's ranking ace, Maj 'Todd' Moore, also scored his final victory of the war. He had added a further two kills to his tally since his 'treble' in late May, and then taken a month's leave. Returning to the 45th FS on 19 July, Moore had failed to encounter the enemy until 10 August, when he led his squadron on a bomber escort mission to Tokyo. Nearing the target, a handful of Japanese fighters attempted to intercept the bombers, but were easily dealt with by the Mustang escorts. Moore destroyed one of the attacking fighters (a 'Tojo') and damaged a further two, taking his final tally to 12.

The various sweeps over Tokyo on the 10th also saw the 506th FG celebrate the crowning of its sole ace, Capt Abner Aust, of the 457th FS. Having downed no fewer than three 'Franks' (and damaged two more) during a swirling dogfight off the coastal city of Tsu, south of Nagoya, late in the afternoon of 16 July, Aust had used his P-51D to destroy a pair of 'Zekes' (with a third damaged) over Tokyo late on the morning of 10 August.

Just 48 hours prior to Japan's Emperor Hirohito announcing his country's unconditional surrender in the aftermath of two devastating atomic bomb attacks on Hiroshima and Nagasaki, VII FC was involved in its last great aerial engagement of a long war. On 13 August 53 P-47Ns from the 507th FG had been sent on Mission 507-35, which basically entailed a sweep over Keijo (now Seoul) in occupied Korea in search of the last remnants of the Japanese Army Air Force. By the time the fighters appeared over the target area, only 38 (12 each from the 463rd and 465th FSs and 14 from the 464th) P-47s remained in the formation.

Arriving over Keijo after more than four hours of flying, the Thunderbolt pilots were rewarded for their powers of endurance with the sight of 50+ enemy aircraft milling around at an altitude of 8000 ft. Over the next 15 minutes, the group would down over 20 enemy aircraft.

The first to fall was a 'Betty' bomber claimed by Capt Ed Hoyt of the 465th FS, this victory being doubly significant for it at last gave the P-47 pilot five kills – Hoyt had downed four aircraft with the 41st FS/35th FG over New Guinea in March 1944 – and produced the 507th FG's first ace. Within minutes the group would have its second.

Having seen the 'Betty' go down, Maj James T Jarman, boss of the 464th FS, spotted what he thought was an 'Oscar' and dived after it, along with his flight. However, before he could engage the fighter, three more appeared from cloud nearby. One of the pilots following his leader into battle was Lt Oscar Perdomo (in P-47N-2 44-88211), who was about to engage an enemy aircraft for the very first time since arriving at Ie Shima in June. The following extracts are taken from his combat report;

Lt Oscar Perdomo and Republic chief test pilot Frank Parker pose for a publicity shot in the wake of the former's 'ace-in-a-day' mission on 13 August 1945 (*Flores*)

Lt Perdomo posing proudly on his victory-adorned P-47N, which he had named in honour of his infant son (*Wolf*)

'I pushed the throttle into water injection with the prop pitch at about 2700 rpm. As I gained on the "Oscars", I placed my gyro sight on the last one and adjusted the sight diamonds on his wings. At this time the "Oscars" were flying in a very loose vee. When I closed into firing range, I gave him a burst and saw my bullets converge on his nose and cockpit. Something exploded in his engine and fire broke out. I was still shooting as he fell to the right.

'I lined up immediately on the second ship and began firing at about 30°. I shot at this "Oscar" until parts flew off and fire broke out on the bottom cowling of his engine. I ceased firing when he rolled over slowly and dived straight into the ground and exploded.'

Having destroyed two fighters in quick succession, Perdomo looked for a third target. He didn't have to search for long;

'I caught him in my fixed sight and led him as much as I could, firing all the way. He continued his spiral turn about 180° until he was about 100 ft off the ground. Then he hit a high-speed stall, because I saw his aircraft shudder, and it snapped him still tighter to the left and into the ground, where he exploded like an oversized napalm bomb.'

With his 'patch of sky' now devoid of aircraft, Perdomo put his aircraft into a climb and headed back toward Keijo in search of 'friendlies'. However, he soon came across two Yokosuka K5Y1 'Willow' navy biplane trainers that seemed to be flying along totally oblivious to the aerial battle taking place around them. The resulting combat was painfully one-sided;

'I picked the closest to me and started shooting. Flames broke out almost immediately. To slow my ship down, I crossed my controls and skidded. Then I shot more rounds at him. This time I must have hit the pilot because the ship went into a spiral to the right and straight into the ground, about 300 ft below.'

The second 'Willow' managed to escape whilst his wingman was being shot down by Perdomo. Having been briefly side-tracked by the two trainers, the American pilot once again headed for Keijo, climbing through cloud as he went. Just as he was breaking through the overcast, a formation of three or four 'Oscars' appeared above him to his right. Sensing that he was tactically disadvantaged, Perdomo immediately turned into them and pushed the nose of his fighter down into a dive – nothing could stay with a heavy P-47 heading earthwards. He hoped that they had not spotted him, but at the last moment they too pushed down in his direction. Selecting water injection, Perdomo soon pulled away from his assailants and banked into nearby cloud, and by the time the enemy fighters attempted to turn after him, the Thunderbolt pilot was already above and behind them;

'As I came in on these "Oscars" three of them turned left and one turned right. I followed this single one and used my gyro sight. His only evasive manoeuvres were turns. I shot at him in bursts until he flamed. He exploded when I pulled alongside because of excessive speed. The mass of flame went into the ground.'

Lt Oscar Perdomo had just become the 507th FG's first, and last, 'ace-in-a-day'. Upon recovery back at Ie Shima after eight hours and eighteen minutes in the

The 45th FS's Maj 'Todd' Moore used this P-51D-20 (44-63483) to score exactly half of his 12 kills

cockpit, the group began to tally up its claims. The 507th FG was credited with 20 destroyed, two probables and one 'Betty' destroyed on the ground for the loss of a solitary P-47, whose pilot (Lt Dallas Yeargain) was made a PoW for a whole two days!

Lt Perdomo's CO, Maj Jarman, later recalled how the unassuming pilot relayed his success to his squadronmates;

'When we landed back at Ie Shima, Perdomo shyly stated that he had destroyed five, including one biplane trainer. Upon developing the gun camera film, it was clearly proven that he had actually destroyed the five aircraft, including the biplane which no one else had even seen.'

Although four of the kills credited to Oscar Perdomo were reported by him to be Ki-43s, postwar research revealed that the quartet of fighters he shot down were actually Ki-84s from the 22nd and 85th Sentais. The Japanese admitted the loss of 11 'Franks' to 'Mustangs', with the CO of the 85th being amongst those killed.

The 507th FG was duly presented with a Distinguished Unit Citation (DUC) for its outstanding performance on 13 August, this being the only such award given to a P-47 group in the Pacific.

On 15 August the Mustang and Thunderbolt pilots continued on their daily business, having little inkling that their sworn enemy would surrender later that day. Indeed, Maj 'Todd' Moore led elements of the 45th FS on a strafing sweep against targets in the Nagoya area, this mission being his 150th combat sortie in 37 months in the Pacific. Upon his return to South Field, on Iwo Jima, he was informed that the war was over.

APPENDICES

P-47 AND P-51 ACES IN THE PACIFIC AND CBI

Southwest Pacific P-47/P-51 Aces

Col Neel E Kearby	22
Maj William Dunham	16
Lt Col William M Banks	9
Capt Walter G Benz	8
Capt LeRoy V Grossheusch	8
Capt Edward Roddy	8
Maj William A Shomo	8
Capt Samuel Blair	7
Lt Marvin Grant	7
Maj John T Moore	7
Capt William H Strand	7
Capt William B Foulis	6
Lt James D Mugavero	6
Lt George Della	5
Lt Michael Dikovitsky	5
Lt Robert Gibb	5
Lt Myron M Hnatio	5
Lt Robert K Knapp	5
Lt Laurence F O'Neill	5
Maj Edward S Popek	5
Maj Robert C Sutcliffe	5
Capt Meade Brown	6

CBI P-51 Aces

Maj John C Herbst	14 (18 in total)
Maj Edward McComas	14
Maj James J England	10
Lt Col Charles Older	8 (18 in total)
Lt Lester L. Arasmith	6
Lt John Bolyard	5
Lt Philip Chapman	5
Lt Robert F Mulhollem	5

Seventh Air Force P-47/P-51 Aces

Maj Robert O Moore	11
Maj James B Tapp	8
Capt Judge E Wolfe	7 (9)
Lt Stanley Lustic	7
Maj Harry L Crim Jr	6
Lt Richard H Andersen	5
Capt Edward R Hoyt	5
Lt William H Mathis	5
Lt Oscar F Perdomo	5
Capt John E Vogt	5

CBI P-51 ACES WITH COMBINED AIR AND GROUND VICTORIES

	Air	Ground	Total WW 2		Air	Ground	Total WW 2
Capt Thomas A Reynolds	3 (1)	25 (6.5)	35.5	Capt John R Branz	1	7	8
Lt Robert E Reed	2	14	16	Capt Chester N Denny	3	5	8
Capt Robert E Brown	2	13	15	Lt James B Harrison	–	7	7
Lt Terry H Wade Jr	2	13	15	Lt Silven E Kosa	–	7	7
Maj Floyd Finberg	3	11	14	Lt Heston C Cole	1	5	6
Lt Ira Binkley	1	11	12	Lt Kenneth G Granger	2	4	6
Lt Louis W Anderson Jr	3	8	11	Lt Nimrod Long	–	6	6
Lt Wesley D Pearson	2	9	11	Lt Hubert Loose	1	5	6
Lt Paul H Swetland	2	9	11	Lt Norman F Niemeier Jr	3	3	6
Maj Grant Mahony	1 (4)	5	10	Lt George T Koran	1.5	4	5.5
Lt Lester E Muenster	1	9	10	Capt Wallace D Cousins	3	2	5
Lt Robert D Wells	1	9	10	Maj Clyde B Slocumb	2	3	5
Lt Warren E Field	4	5.5	9.5	Lt William H McKinney	1	4	5
Lt John C Conn	4	5	9	Lt Charles W Perelka	–	5	5
Capt Lauren A Howard	–	9	9				

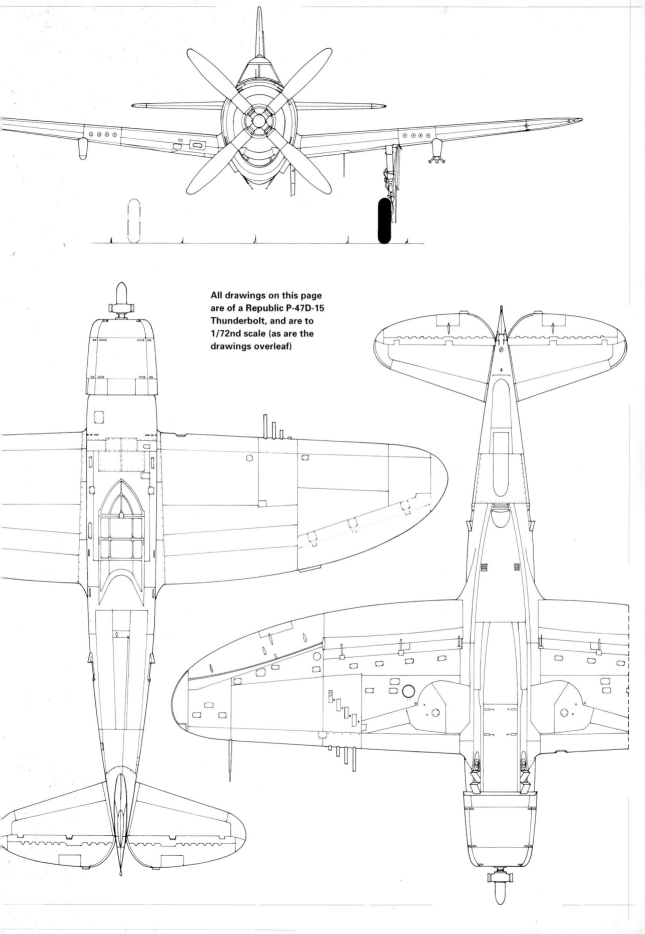

All drawings on this page
are of a Republic P-47D-15
Thunderbolt, and are to
1/72nd scale (as are the
drawings overleaf)

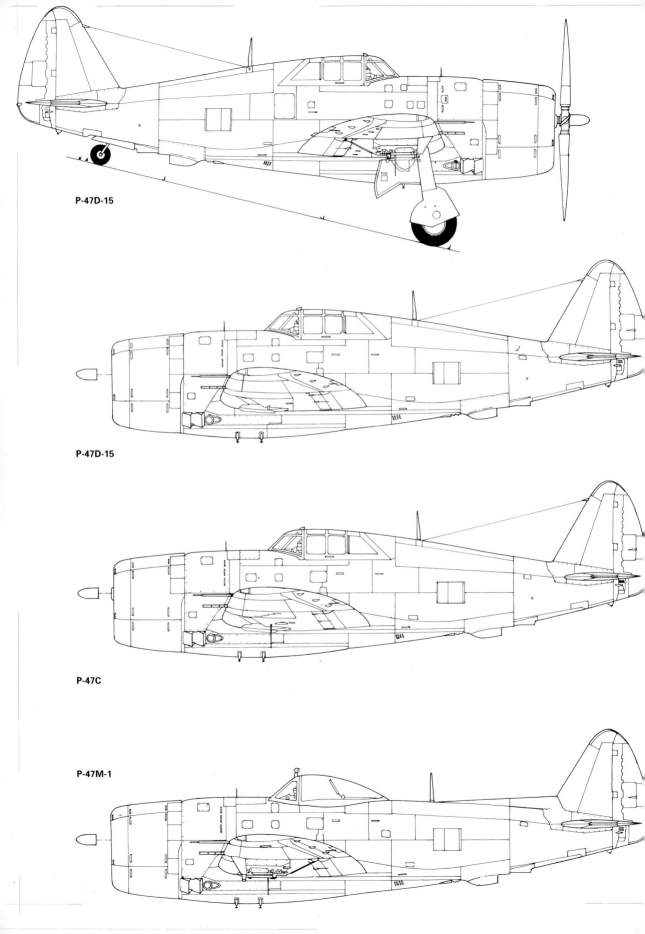

P-47D-15

P-47D-15

P-47C

P-47M-1

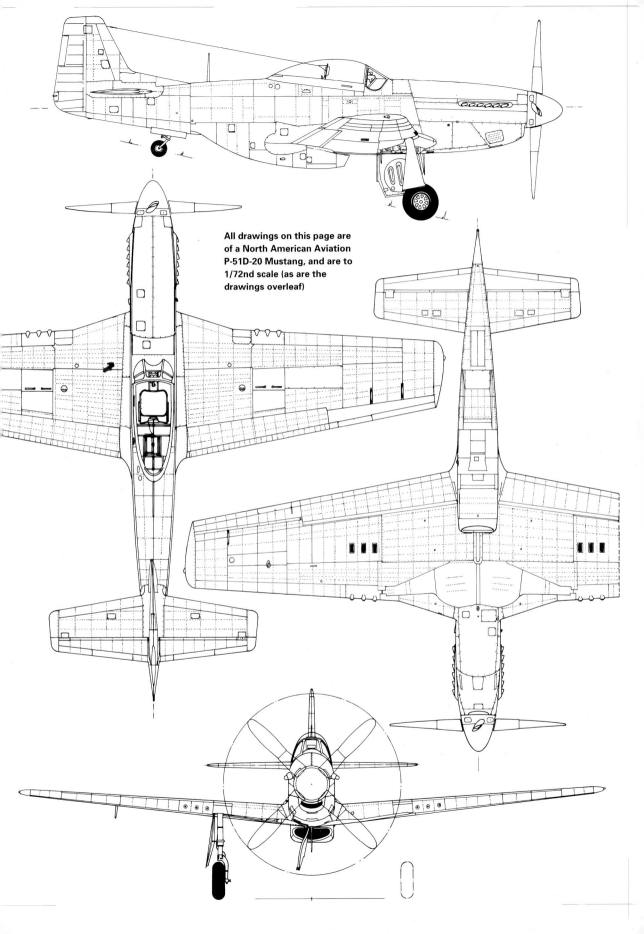

All drawings on this page are
of a North American Aviation
P-51D-20 Mustang, and are to
1/72nd scale (as are the
drawings overleaf)

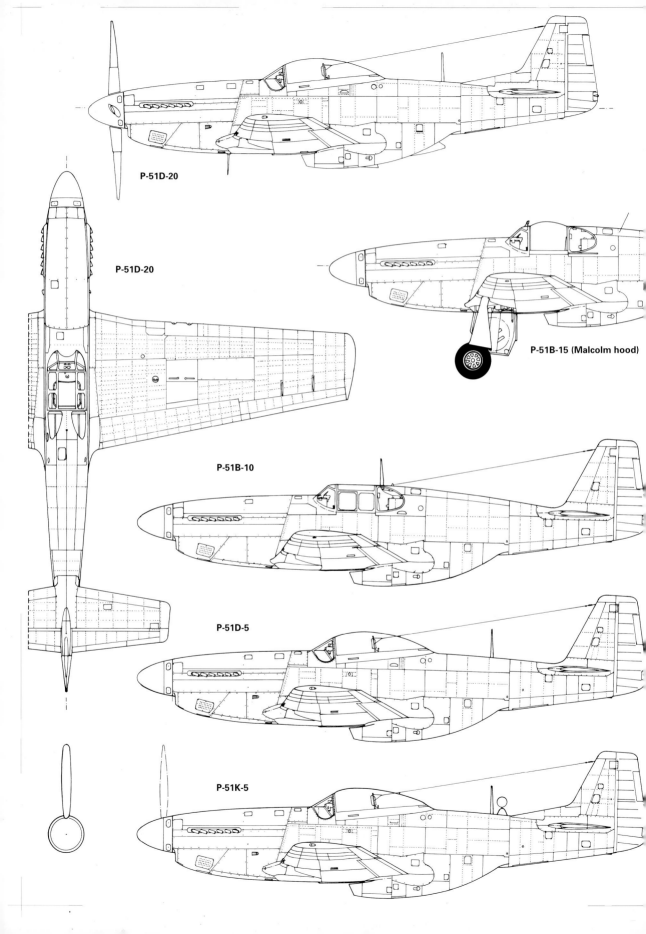

P-51D-20

P-51D-20

P-51B-15 (Malcolm hood)

P-51B-10

P-51D-5

P-51K-5

1

P-47D-2 42-8145/*Firey Ginger* of Lt Col Neel Ernest Kearby, CO of the 348th FG, Port Moresby, July-September 1943

Neel Kearby teamed up with this D-2 (note the mis-spelling of 'fiery', which was corrected on his subsequent P-47s) soon after arriving in New Guinea with the 348th FG in May 1943. According to informal reports of his early actions, he gained his first three victories in this machine in September, before using a second D-2 christened *Fiery Ginger III* on his Medal of Honor mission on 11 October. The first *Fiery Ginger* was actually used by Kearby during the group's early months of training in the USA in 1942/43, and the P-47 shown here should have actually been christened *Fiery Ginger II* – Kearby chose this name in honour of his wife, Virginia. Late in November 1943, *Fiery Ginger III* was passed to the recently-arrived 58th FG, Kearby completing his tally of 22 kills using P-47D-4 42-22668 *Fiery Ginger IV*.

2

P-47D-2 42-8096/*Miss Mutt*/*PRIDE OF LODI OHIO* of Lt Col William Richard Rowland, Deputy CO of the 348th FG, Port Moresby, November 1943

Rowland definitely used this D-2 to score his fourth and fifth victories on 7 November, and may have indeed used it to secure his three previous kills. He often led the 348th FG into combat when Neel Kearby was not on operations, and consequently scored on the days when his boss had stood down.

3

P-47D-2 42-8067/*Bonnie* of Capt William Dunham, 342nd FS/348th FG, Port Moresby, October-December 1943

'Dinghy' Dunham and Neel Kearby were great friends from their days together patrolling the Panama Protection Zone in P-39s with the 14th Pursuit Squadron/53rd Pursuit Group. This D-2 was almost certainly used by the future ace to gain his first seven victories. According to group records, most of the 348th FG's D-2s had been replaced by D-4s come January 1944.

4

P-47D-4 42-22684/*Miss Mutt II*/*PRIDE OF LODI OHIO* of Lt Col William Richard Rowland, CO of the 348th FG, Finschhafen, December 1943

Miss Mutt II replaced Lt Col Rowland's D-2 (seen in profile 2) sometime towards the end of November or the beginning of December 1943. According to eyewitnesses, the CO of the 348th FG subsequently scored his remaining trio of victories during the course of the next few months whilst flying this aircraft. His final kill was achieved on 27 February, and from then on group duties prevented him from adding to his score. Controversy surrounds his last victory, which took the form of a Ki-21 bomber that had initially been attacked by Neel Kearby. Seemingly mortally damaged by the ace's fire, the aircraft's final moments were being recorded by Rowland using his gun camera when he noticed it level out just above the ground and attempt to fly off. His quick reactions prevented any such escape for the bomber, however, and it was swiftly downed.

5

P-47D-11 42-22903/"*Kathy*"/*VENI VIDI VICI* of Lt Lawrence O'Neill, 342nd FS/348th FG, Finschhafen, December 1943

Lt O'Neill had the unique distinction (for a P-47 pilot in New Guinea at least) of scoring all five of his victories against G4M 'Betty' bombers. Having downed a solitary example on 13 September, he was credited with destroying no fewer than four navy bombers over New Britain on 26 December whilst protecting the Allied invasion force landing at Cape Gloucester. The P-47D-2 that he used on this occasion was described by him as being 'unusually balky', and it groundlooped when O'Neill landed back at Finschhafen. Thankful to be alive, he was left to spectate alongside his forlorn fighter as the rest of his squadron-mates buzzed the airfield in celebration of the day's successes.

6

P-47D-4 (serial unknown) of Maj Gerald R Johnson, CO of the 9th FS/49th FG, Nadzab, January 1944

The P-47 was not popular with the formerly P-38-equipped 9th FS primarily because of its limited range and sluggish handling qualities below 18,000 ft. However, the 9th soldiered on with the Thunderbolt between November 1943 and February 1944, and several aces scored in the type. The unit's CO, 'Jerry' Johnson, was one of those to claim kills, downing a 'Tony' on 10 December 1943 and a 'Zeke' on 18 January 1944. Note that the white area below the cockpit is masking applied by the groundcrew in preparation for the application of Johnson's kill decals.

7

P-47D-3 42-22637/*DARING DOTTIE III* of Maj John T Moore, CO of the 341st FS/348th FG, Finschhafen, March 1944

John Moore scored his final four victories (out of a total of seven) in this aircraft, the last of which took the form of a 'Zeke' off Manus Island on 2 March 1944. Early photos of 42-22637 suggest that the fighter was conventionally camouflaged at some point, prior to adopting this unique scheme, the purpose of which has never been explained. After completing his stint as 341st FS CO in July 1944, John Moore was transferred to the group's HQ Flight, and remained here until lost in action on 8 October during a dive-bombing mission over Ceram Island, west of New Guinea, in P-47D-23 42-27596.

8

P-47D-4 42-22668/*Fiery Ginger IV* of Col Neel E Kearby, V Fighter Command, Finschhafen, March 1944

The mystery surrounding the identity of Neel Kearby's mount on his last mission never seems to flag. Some 348th FG veterans remember Kearby using Capt Jesse Ivey's P-47 on the fatal mission, but the serial number found in March 1946 on the wrecked tail fin section of the fighter which carried the colonel to his death corresponds with that worn by *FIERY GINGER IV*. However, included in this volume is a photo of a P-47 displaying 22 victory marks beneath its cockpit, implying that 42-22668 was still in existence *after* the mission on which Kearby was lost – he scored his 22nd, and last, victory just moments before being shot down. Until someone comes up with foolproof evidence to the contrary, this profile must be considered to be the most accurate image yet produced of the P-47 flown by Kearby from the end of 1943 until his death on 5 March 1944.

9

P-47D-11 42-22855/*HOYT'S HOSS* of Lt Edward R Hoyt, 41st FS/35th FG, Gusap, March 1944

Hoyt scored all four of his V FC victories during March of 1944 in

APPENDICES

this aircraft, claiming a quartet of 'Oscars' between the 11th and 14th. He then had to wait until 13 August 1945 to 'make ace', claiming a 'Betty' bomber over Korea in a P-47N whilst flying with the 465th FS/507th FG – he completed 14 VLRs with the group in the last two months of the war.

10

P-47D-2 42-22532/*Sunshine III* of Capt W M Banks, CO of the 342nd FS/348th FG, Finschhafen, February-June 1944

Bill Banks almost certainly used this late-build D-2 to down some, if not all, of his five kills in New Guinea in 1943. However, he certainly did not use it to destroy his sixth confirmed victory over Cape Gloucester on 7 February 1944, for by that time he had been issued with a P-47D-3. Banks failed to score again until participating in the retaking of the Philippines (in a P-47D-23) in late 1944, by which time he had been promoted to the rank of major and posted to the HQ Flight of the 348th FG.

11

P-51A-10 43-6189 of Col Phillip Cochran, CO of the 1st Air Commando Group, Hailakandi, March-May 1944

Although not technically an ace, Col Phillip G Cochran deserves a mention in this volume for he was the CO of the 1st ACG from its formation on 29 March 1944 until the group received a Distinguished Unit Citation in mid-May 1944. During this time it had heavily involved in supporting Orde Wingate's 'Chindit Raiders', who were operating behind enemy lines in Burma. Prior to arriving in India to take command of the pioneer air commando group, Cochran had been credited with the destruction of two enemy aircraft in North Africa, although his Burma assignment failed to produce opportunities for additional claims.

12

P-47D-23 43-27899/*JOSIE* of Lt Mike Dikovitsky, 340th FS/348th FG, Leyte, December 1944

Apparently one the first D-23s issued to the 348th, this aircraft enjoyed a long career with the group which spanned a good nine months of 1944. Assigned to Mike Dikovitsky for much of this time, it is likely that he scored his final three (of five) kills in this very fighter. The first of these was downed over Wewak on 11 March, whilst the second and third were claimed in December in the Philippines – by which time the 348th had adopted its distinctive black fuselage recognition bands, as seen here.

13

P-51A-1 43-6077/*Jackie* of Capt James John England, 530th FS/311th FG, Dinjan, May 1944

This well-worn P-51A-1 could undoubtedly boast the most distinguished record of any Allison-engined Mustang used by the USAAF in World War 2. Originally delivered wearing the script *SPIRIT OF UNIVERSAL* in honour of the workers of the Universal Engineering Company of Frankensmith, Michigan (who had raised the funds necessary to pay for its construction), was renamed *Jackie* by James England in honour of his wife, Jaqueline, soon after it was issued to his unit in India in late 1943. Photo records from the period suggest that the individual squadron number '75' was added sometime after he had scored a number of his kills, many of which were not recorded on *Jackie*. This theory is supported by the fact that the aircraft displays just two of his many victories claimed in A-models between November 1943 and May 1944 – indeed, only three of

England's kills (on 11 and 14 May) have so far been traced to this particular aircraft. However, certain squadron records indicate that all eight Burma kills credited to the 311th FG's ranking ace were scored in this very fighter, although further documentation shows that his first two victories (on 25 and 27 November 1943) were achieved flying a P-51A-10! One thing is for certain, however – squadronmate, Lt William Griffith, won the Silver Star flying this veteran Mustang in China in late 1944.

14

P-47D-21 43-25343/*Joey* of Lt William Mathis, 19th FS/318th FG, Saipan, June 1944

One of the first D-21s built by Republic, it is likely that this is the aircraft Mathis flew off one of the two aircraft carriers that transported the 19th FS (along with the rest of the 318th FG) to Saipan in June 1944. Once ashore, it joined the remaining 72 P-47Ds in flying ground support missions for the battle-weary Marines fighting their way across Saipan and nearby Tinian. There is no record of 43-25343 ever being engaged in combat with Japanese aircraft, and all five fighters credited to William Mathis were claimed in May-June 1945 in a P-47N-1.

15

P-47D-23 43-27861 of Lt LeRoy V Grossheusch, 39th FS/35th FG, Morotai, September 1944

This P-47 was almost certainly allocated to Grossheusch in June 1944, and flown by him until year end – by which time he had become CO of the 39th FS. Following his promotion, Grossheusch enjoyed a 'purple patch' in combat, downing six aircraft between 30 January and 25 February 1945 flying a P-47N.

16

P-51C (serial unknown) *Little Jeep* of Capt Forrest H Parham, 75th FS/23rd FG, Luliang, November 1944

Canadian-born 'Pappy' Parham was an 'old hand' with the 75th FS by the time he scored his final two kills with this P-51C to 'make ace' in November 1944. His previous three victories had come on the P-40N in August/September 1944, and he had been flying in China since the beginning of the year. Parham was subsequently shot down by flak whilst strafing Lungwha airfield in P-51D-5 44-11312 on 2 April 1945, although he successfully evaded capture and returned to his unit 23 days later.

17

P-51C (serial/sub-type unknown) *LOPE'S HOPE 3rd* of Lt Don S Lopez, 75th FS/23rd FG, Kweilin, September 1944

Don Lopez was yet another 75th FS pilot to 'make ace' on the P-51C after scoring his first kills on the 'better' P-40N, which he considered superior to the Mustang when it came to air combat on the China front. *LOPE'S HOPE 3rd* was used by its namesake to damage an 'Oscar' on 16 September 1944 and destroy a Ki-43 – for his fifth straight 'Oscar' victory – on 11 November.

18

P-51B-7 (probably 43-7060) *Tommy's Dad* of Maj John C Herbst, CO of the 74th FS/23rd FG, Luliang, January 1945

'Pappy' Herbst started his incredible scoring run in this aircraft on 3 September 1944 when he downed two 'Vals'. A further 11 victories, one probable and one damaged would be claimed by the joint ranking ace of the China front, the last of these falling on 17 January 1945. Boasting a final score of 18, Herbst downed four of his remaining victories in P-40s and claimed a sole kill (and one damaged) in another Mustang aside from *Tommy's Dad*. The solitary swastika victory marking applied to the aircraft signified a Bf 109 that Herbst reportedly claimed whilst flying in the MTO, although exact details of this kill have yet to surface. Despite being the most famous Mustang in the CBI, questions remain as to the exact identity of this aircraft. Most evidence points to it being 43-7060, which was built as a P-51B-5 but later became one of 550 aircraft of this sub-type upgraded to B-7 specs following the fitment of an additional fuselage fuel tank.

19

P-51C (serial/sub-type unknown) *IOWA BELLE* of Lt Curtiss W Mahanna, 75th FS/23rd FG, Luliang, January 1945
Like Lopez and Parham, Curtiss Mahanna also enjoyed some success with the P-51 once the 75th FS had at last converted from the Warhawk to the Mustang. He claimed an 'Oscar' and a 'Tojo' on 11 November 1944, and then downed another Ki-43 on 14 January 1945. The scores on these two dates represented his sum total of combat victories during the war, as Japanese opposition in the air became hard to come by as 1945 wore on.

20

P-47D-23 42-27886/*Sylvia*/*Racine Belle* of Lt M E Grant, 342nd FS/348th FG, Leyte, November 1944-January 1945
This unusually-marked Thunderbolt carries kill markings for all seven of Lt Grant's confirmed victories, which he had scored in earlier aircraft by mid-June 1944. The aircraft was used by Grant in the Philippines until he transferred out of the unit at the end of January 1945. The red and white stripe along the fuselage was an ID marking introduced by the 342nd FS in late 1944.

21

P-47D-25 42-28110/*My Baby* of Capt Alvaro Jay Hunter, 40th FS/35th FG, Pitoe, December 1944-January 1945
Hunter used this P-47 during his final weeks with the 40th FS whilst based at Pitoe air station, on Morotai. Late in January 1945 the unit was transferred to Luzon, in the Philippines, and this Thunderbolt almost certainly made the trip north. Hunter, however, did not, for he had completed his tour on 10 January and had been sent home. Note that the pilot's *My Baby* nickname was inscribed on both sides of this aircraft, and it also wore the familiar 'USAAC' rudder markings.

22

P-47D-25, 42-27894/*Bonnie* of Maj William D Dunham, CO of the 460th FS/348th FG, Leyte, December 1944
As the 348th FG's second most successful ace, 'Dinghy' Dunham almost certainly scored his final four P-47 kills in this particular fighter. Dunham left his beloved 460th FS in mid-December to become assistant group ops officer, prior to returning home in January 1945 to attend a gunnery course. By the time he rejoined the group in May, its P-47s had been replaced by P-51s (the first examples had arrived in February).

23

P-47D-28 42-28505/*My Baby* of Capt Alvaro Jay Hunter, 40th FS/35th FG, October-December 1944
This aircraft was Jay Hunter's personal mount for his final months in combat with the 40th FS. A veteran of 184 missions stretching back to September 1943, when his unit was

equipped with P-39Q-6s, Hunter scored his final trio of victories in a P-47 in October/November 1944. All five of his victims were flying 'Oscar' fighters. Hunter briefly commanded the 40th FS from 8 November to 8 December 1944, although this was only a temporary measure due to his imminent posting back to the USA. Note that this aircraft carried the *My Baby* titling on the right side of its fuselage only, and had had the group's distinctive 'USAAC' rudder stripes either weathered or scraped off.

24

F-6D-10 44-14841/*SNOOKS-5th* of Capt William Shomo, CO of the 82nd TRS/71st TRG, Leyte, January 1945
Shomo used this F-6D to down seven aircraft in one mission on 11 January 1945. It is also depicted in Iain Wyllie's cover art, although it lacks the yellow fin tip marking in the specially-commissioned painting, as this was added after Shomo's legendary sortie. Although not stated in the unit's documentation, or in the pilot's log book, it would seem likely that he also used this aircraft to down his only other kill, claimed 24 hours earlier.

25

P-51D-20 44-72505 *The FLYING UNDERTAKER* of Maj William Shomo, CO of the 82nd TRS/71st TRG, Binmaley, February-April 1945
With *SNOOKS-5th* temporarily out of action following damage from flying debris shed by some of William Shomo's seven victims on 11 January, the boss of the 82nd TRS was issued with this near-new P-51D-20 in its place. US war corespondents quickly seized on the pilot's unusual peacetime employment, and it was probably due to their pestering that he adopted the previously unused nickname of *The FLYING UNDERTAKER* for this aircraft. Well photographed over the ensuing months, the P-51 was kept in almost spotless condition throughout this time.

26

P-51D-20 44-63984/*Margaret IV* of Maj James Buckley Tapp, CO of the 78th FS/15th FG, Iwo Jima (South Field), April-May 1945
One of the longest-serving members of the 78th FS, Jim Tapp joined the unit in late 1942 and remained with it through to war's end. His first *Margarets* were a series of P-40s, but in late 1944 the name was used to adorn a far deadlier fighter – a P-51D-20. In early 1945 he led the 78th FS to Iwo Jima, and from there the unit flew a number of highly successful VLR sorties as escorts for B-29s bombing Japan between April and VJ-Day. It was during the early missions that Tapp scored six of his eight kills in this aircraft – the final two were claimed in a P-51D-25 in late May.

27

P-51D-20 44-63483/*Stinger VII* of Maj Robert W Moore, 45th FS/15th FG, Iwo Jima (South Field), June 1945
Top ace of the Seventh Air Force, 'Todd' Moore scored his first victory in a P-40N on 26 January 1944, but subsequently claimed his remaining 11 kills in the P-51D. Six of these fell to the guns of *Stinger VII*, which replaced an earlier D-20 upon his posting to the 45th FS in late May. He duly became the CO of this unit on 19 July, and remained its boss through to VJ-Day.

28

P-51D (serial/sub-type unknown) of Maj C B Slocumb, CO of the 75th FS/23rd FG, Luliang, April-August 1945

A veteran of two combat tours (he served with the 16th FS/51st FG in Indian and China in 1942-43), Clyde Slocumb commanded the 75th FS from November 1944 through to VJ-Day. A man who led by example, the major quickly reversed the sagging morale of his new unit – its pilots were less than happy about seeing their P-40Ns replaced by P-51Cs. Despite his vigorous leadership qualities, Slocumb was never shot down in combat, although he was forced to bail out of a P-51D on 2 April near Hainan airfield when its engine quit. In typical style, he returned to his unit 23 days later via a Chinese junk! Credited in several postwar aces' listings with seven kills, it is now widely believed that Slocumb scored two aerial victories (one in a P-40E) at most, plus three ground kills. This particular P-51D was flown by him during the last months of the conflict in China.

29

P-51B-15 42-106908 of Lt Leonard R Reeves, 530th FS/311th FG, Pungchacheng, January 1945

'Randy' Reeves flew this Mustang on at least one occasion, and it was almost certainly his regular mount before it was named MY DALLAS DARLIN by him. This Mustang suffered severe tail damage during one of the two Peking missions flown around 25 January, resulting in Reeves being assigned another P-51.

30

P-51C-10 42-103285/JANIE of Lt Lester Muenster, 530th FS/311th FG, Pungchacheng, January 1945

Muenster scored his one aerial victory (an 'Oscar') near Sinsiang airfield on 5 January 1945 in this P-51 – a further five Japanese fighters fell to other 530th FS pilots that same day, including three 'Oscars' credited to Leonard Reeves, giving him ace status. Muenster was also credited with nine ground victories.

31

P-51D-10 44-14626 of Lt Col Edward O McComas, CO of the 118th TRS/23rd FG, Luliang, January 1945

All of the kills that McComas tallied were scored in P-51Cs, and he almost certainly received this P-51D late in December 1944 or early in January 1945 – just prior to completing his tour.

32

P-51D-10 44-11276 of Lt Col Charles H Older, 23rd FG, Luliang, June 1945

Older was already an ace with the AVG when he went home after the group disbanded in July 1942. He subsequently joined the USAAF and returned to China exactly two years later to take command of the 76th FS/23rd FG. Older scored his first Mustang kill with this unit on 28 July 1944, whilst his remaining seven P-51 victories came after he had moved to the group's HQ flight. By the time he was issued with this aircraft, Older was serving as Deputy Group CO – hence the fuselage stripes.

33

P-51K-10 44-12099/JOSIE of Lt Michael Dikovitsky, 340th FS/348th FG, San Marcelino, January 1945

All of Dikovitsky's victories had been gained in P-47s prior to the 340th transitioning to the P-51 early in 1945, and he rotated home in March 1945 having had little opportunity to use the Mustang in combat. Note the swirl of red and white on the propeller spinner, which was probably a personal 'touch' added by 340th FS veterans rather than an actual squadron marking.

34

P-51K-10 44-12101/Nadine of Capt George Della, 460th FS/348th FG, Floridablance, May-June 1945

George Della also scored his five victories in P-47s. The 460th FS had completed its transition to the Mustang by late March 1945 – too late for air action over the Philippines, but in time for the final assault on Japan itself. Della missed the final blows dealt to the empire, however, for he rotated home in June 1945.

35

P-51K-10 44-12073/SUNSHINE VII of Lt Col William T Banks, CO of the 348th FG, Ie Shima, July 1945

Lt Col Banks had scored all nine of his kills by the end of December 1944 flying P-47Ds. Bearing his full scoreboard, this P-51K was one of the most strikingly-marked of all Pacific fighters, for it also carried a multi-striped spinner as per standard group commanders' practice at this stage of the war. Each quadrant denoted a unit within the group – black for the 460th, blue for the 342nd, yellow for the 341st and red for the 340th. The fighter's nickname was also interlaced with squadron colours.

36

P-51D-20 44-75623/My Ach'in! of Maj Harry C Crim, CO of the 531st FS/21st FG, Iwo Jima, July 1945

Maj Crim had completed a tour in the MTO on P-38s prior to taking command of the 531st FS on Iwo Jima at the end of March 1945. The unusual nickname on of his Mustang referred to the deadening effect the dauntingly long VLR missions to Japan had on the seat of his trousers! He scored his last victory during a sweep on Japan on 6 July 1945, taking his tally to six confirmed and 5.25 damaged during those stultifyingly long missions.

37

P-51D-20 44-64038/Doris Marie of Lt Thomas Sheets, 460th FS/348th FG, Ie Shima, August 1945

Lt Sheets is listed with three confirmed and two probable victories in wartime accounts, his final kill being scored during the 348th's last aerial engagement on 1 August 1945. He was originally credited with two kills for that day over Kyushu, but subsequent examination reduced one claim to a probable. He is also credited with an 'Oscar' on 29 November 1944 and a 'Sally' on 7 December 1944 – both over the Philippines. Note that Sheets's Mustang sports the 460th FS's black ram insignia.

38

P-51K-10 44-12017/ "MRS. BONNIE" of Lt Col William D Dunham, 348th FG, Ie Shima, August 1945

'Dinghy' Dunham was Deputy Group CO during the final months of the war, and he scored his 16th, and last, kill in this aircraft on 1 August 1945 when he downed a Ki-84 over Kyushu.

39

P-47N-1 44-88211/Lil Meaties' MEAT CHOPPER of Lt Oscar Perdomo, 464th FS/507th FG, Ie Shima, August 1945

Lt Perdomo arrived with the 507th on Ie Shima in June 1945, and flew his first mission on 2 July. There was little chance for the 507th to meet the Japanese in the air, especially after the atomic bombings, but on 13 August 38 507th P-47Ns encountered 50 Japanese aircraft over the Korean capital, and the chase began. In the subsequent melee, Oscar Perdomo downed five aircraft in this P-47N , thus making him the last